SANDY

AND

GARBO

Chuck "Garbo" Hajinian

'This book is dedicated to

"The Ancient of Days"

who created such beautiful animals

to bless our lives.'

First published by Dog Ear Publishing
4010 W. 86th Street, Ste H
Indianapolis, IN 46268
www.dogearpublishing.net

dog ear
PUBLISHING

ISBN: 978-159858-300-7

This book is printed on acid-free paper.
This book is a true story. Some names have been changed.

Printed in the United States of America

TABLE OF CONTENTS

SANDY AND GARBO

"The fire was raging through the field across the street. Grabbing my garden hose, I ran as fast as I could. You know Garbo, a three-hundred-pound guy like me doesn't move that fast. This foolish neighbor had let a small, leaf-burning fire get out of control, and now the field next to his house was ablaze, threatening to consume the house!" John paused to take a deep breath and continue with his story. "Most of the neighbors had brought over their hoses and were attempting to put the fire out. I was standing there, trying to catch my breath from the run when all of a sudden, I get this blunt punch right in the butt. I ignore it and continue spraying water. Again a poke, this time in the upper thigh. The third poke is quite painful, you know where. Angrily, I turn around and there is Sandy, her big yellow Labrador tail wagging while her tongue hung out of her smiling face. She knew what she was doing. I had tied her chain to a log to keep her home. Dragging the chain and log 100 yards, she obviously didn't want to miss the action. There she was, just showing off to all of the neighbors. We eventually got the fire out and I carried the log back home with Sandy in tow."

John would continue, his apple red cheeks reflecting the setting sun at the lake party, "Labrador Retrievers are always torn between pleasing their master and having their own way."

There were many stories at the party. Practically the whole neighborhood was at my house. Like one big family, drinking, eating and telling "Sandy" stories. It wasn't always like that. There was a time when most of the neighbors didn't know each other. Their busy lives kept them indifferent to the rest of the people next door and around our fifteen home cul-de-sac. That all changed due to a yellow Lab named Sandy.

Dogs can steal your heart. They take on human qualities. They require the care of a child and can get in more trouble then a rambunctious three-year-old. Canines were too much care and work for me. Knowing all the challenges, my daughters' main goal was to get a dog. They knew all the great things about growing up with a dog. Convincing me, their dad, became their battle cry.

Garbo, I like the idea of writing our memoirs, but I'm really too busy for a book. So, here's the deal. You write the story and I'll insert my comments in *bold print* when I feel the need to say a few words... from a dog's point of view. Deal? Deal! Gotta run! Your Labrador buddy, Sandy!

CHAPTER 1

Stacy's One Big Wish

Leiney and Dune

"A dog? Why on earth would we get a dog?" Seven years ago, this was my reaction to joining the millions of others who have opened their homes to these four-legged canine friends. Everyone had a friend who had a dog, or had one themselves. Owning a dog is a part of being an American. We shoot off fireworks on the Fourth of July, we value our freedom, and we all have dog stories to tell from our past.

I had one as a kid growing up. He was a purebred beagle named Patches. Coming from a long line of National field champions, we knew more about his ancestors then we did about our own family. Some breeder took the time to write all of this down: This great grandmother won this national trophy and this great grandfather won that international hunting trophy. It went on and on. Buying Patches with my dad and sister was a college class for corporate purchasing agents.

When it came to buying something, my Armenian dad always had to have a deal so he could sleep at night. Yes, he was born in this country and fought the Japanese in World War II, but he, like most American-Armenians, held onto the teachings, stories and wisdom of the 'old country'. This wisdom was passed down from his parents and grandparents. This Armenian culture was ingrained into our

American thinking, now three generations removed from the distant villages. It was simply in our blood.

My dad grew up during the Great Depression. From 1929 until, some say, the start of World War II in 1940, the Great Depression was a time of economic uncertainty. Unlike today, when most people can go out and buy what they like or need, some days during that period, you barely had food. Only our grandparents remember those days. People who lived through the Great Depression respect money. For American-Armenians of that era, money is to be saved for the rainy day that never comes. Then you die and your grandchildren buy $200 video game cartridges.

Like the Jews, most of the time the Armenians found themselves exiled from their homeland by some of the big armies of the last two thousand years. Starting with the Romans and ending with the Ottomans, famous guys such as Genghis Khan and Tamerlane were riding into Armenian villages with destruction, rape and pillage on their minds.

During that time we Armenians had to think on our feet, simply because we were usually running and carrying everything that we owned with us. Obviously, under those conditions we learned to live by this idiom: NEVER PAY RETAIL!

My dad listened patiently to all this pedigree and the famous ancestors of the dog. The longer the pitch, the higher the price. This he knew. After a pause, the breeder announced with a haughty smile the fee: around two hundred and seventy-five dollars. This was a lot of money for the 1960's. After he was given the price, he quietly put his Kleenex up to his large Armenian nose, paused and said, "What do you have for fifty dollars?"

The breeder jerked his head back as if hit by a stiff wind. His eyes rolled around in his head like a pinwheel. This breeder was short-circuiting. Rarely would someone challenge a pedigree dog fee. Pausing a moment, he went to the litter searching for some special pup. My younger sister and I looked at each other. My six-year-old sister had worked so hard to convince my dad to look for a dog. Notes and cut-out dog pictures decorated our refrigerator for years. Tears were welling up in the corners of her eyes. Would these two grown ups come up with a deal? We had been disappointed in the past. I grew up on stories of how my dad's family could not afford a Christmas tree during the Great Depression. Western Christianity celebrated Christmas Day on December 25th. Eastern Christianity, which included the Armenians, celebrated the holiday on January 6th. No one can explain why the change came. Perhaps it had something to do with the after-Christmas sales. My dad and grandparents would wait until the Odars or non-Armenians threw their old Christmas trees into the alley. Then they would pick one up, put candles on it and celebrate Armenian Christmas.

I asked my dad if he and his sisters lit the candles on those dry trees.

His response was terse. "We were poor, but not stupid!"

By now my daydream was interrupted by a beagle puppy placed into my sister's arms. Our eyes were wide open with excitement as he scampered to get free. He had a certain flaw, which the breeder explained to us. On his left leg, his claw did not make it down to his paw. It would kind of sit there all of his life on his 'ankle'. I knew my dad would never pay an entrance fee for a National Beagle Dog Contest, so who cared about a claw? Dad got the deal of the century; we got our dog. My sister's soft tears coated the dog's soft fur. We named him 'Patches' because of his brown, white and tan coat. Bragging rights would be ours as we explained to our friends and relatives, pinky finger turned up, "his mother and grandmother were national field champions."

For centuries, Beagles were one of the finest hunting breeds known to man. Patches was a great dog, but had a hunting problem. He couldn't smell a rabbit ten feet away. All that breeding didn't help him. My sister and I would turn his head so he could *see* the rabbit. Then he would explode into a loud howl that would raise his front paws off the pavement. We, of course, struggled to hold him back after the rabbit was long gone. Dad would just sit there in his aluminum lounge chair with the polyester support strips, which had enough give to be comfortable. While puffing his cigar away, he watched this dog sniff around the yard, oblivious to a rabbit quietly shaking a few feet away. Deep inside he knew he'd gotten a great deal, and that is all that mattered to him.

Those were great times, but adulthood had knocked a bit more common sense into me than I had at the age of ten. Dogs are similar to messy children, and my wife and I already had four of those. My time was spent building up a busy dental practice. Free time was occupied by yard work on our one-acre lake home and breaking up fights between my three daughters and one son. Plus, dogs cost money. Food, toys, grooming, vet visits—it all adds up. Not to mention all the training for dogs and kids. Mentally, you have to be ready for a puppy. I wasn't.

Most dads will tell you, though, that no matter how much common sense you have and how hard you're standing strong, there is one thing that can make you just melt: DAUGHTERS. Especially daughters that have that 'neck and face down' look to an art. You know, that "I'm-your-sweet-little-princess-and-I'll-never-love-another-man-more-than-you-Daddy. If-you-just-let-me-have-my-way" look. It was my persistent middle daughter, Stacy, who finally broke down the barriers to get her one big wish.

It all started on a quiet Monday night after a long and cold Wisconsin winter day; our family sat watching television. What else can you do when it is twenty degrees outside? Suddenly, an image of a large animal appeared at the darkened patio doors. We jumped and as our collective eyes focused, we discovered a large yellow Labrador dog with her tongue hanging out. She watched us as her head moved side-to-side opposite to her wagging tail.

Her name was Leiney, short for the Wisconsin-made beer Leinenkugal. My three daughters 12, 9, 6 and a 15-year-old son, jumped to the window amazed that this dog would visit us! A moment or two later, Leiney was gone, disappearing into the cold, star-filled Wisconsin winter night.

The genie was out of the bottle! This revived a secret wish as Stacy exclaimed, "I want a dog. Please, Dad, please!"

Stacy was our one hundred percent kid. She was a perfectionist and everything she took to task, she accomplished. Through perseverance, she could reach any goal. On and off over two years, we would have this discussion about acquiring a dog. Stacy was very patient. Like waiting for Christmas Day while looking at all the presents, Stacy counted her days.

Leiney would continue to visit us and sometimes the girls would get to pet her. But, who was this dog and who did she belong to?

After inquiring with John, our neighbor next door, we discovered that Leiney belonged to the young bachelor down the street named Pete. There was plenty of room for Leiney to roam the neighborhood. Pete would later explain that Leiney had the wanderlust that comes with the Labrador breed. They are bred to be hunters and retrievers. The breed is the finest dogs for flushing out birds and retrieving hunted ducks, all with the sight of a hand signal or small whistle. They love to be in front of a group of hunters "quartering" back and forth until they flush out a pheasant. When hunters take out their guns and get their hunting jackets on, these dogs go crazy with excitement.

Labradors are the most popular breed in America. It seems that every family has either a yellow, chocolate or black Lab. Our cul-de-sac street had three Labs at one time. All were kept inside or in an outdoor kennel. All except Leiney. Actually, that is not completely true- Leiney was kept in an outdoor kennel when Pete went to work.

Upon returning, Pete would find Leiney lying in her kennel looking peaceful and innocent. His answering machine told a different story: "Hello, this is the Delafield police. We found your dog about a mile away at the McDonald's restaurant and put her back into your kennel."

Another message left two hours later by a stranger from downtown Delafield: "Hello, we found your Lab and put her back in her kennel following the address and phone number on her collar."

Pete got to know the manager at the local McDonald's restaurant. The typical call went like this: "Hi Pete. This is Joe. I got Leiney up here. We found her in the ladies' restroom!"

Pete would just sigh, get in his car and go capture his wanderer. The next day, she ended up in the men's room.

Leiney had discovered how to climb a five-foot cyclone fence and escape. When Pete put plywood and rocks on it, she would pound it until the rocks rolled off and then would climb out. If that didn't work, she simply burrowed her way through the dirt and would escape to explore food treasures in neighborhood garages.

8

Pete did not want to be shown up by the dog. As the neighbors watched, he put cyclone fence around the ground butting up to the cage. Then he put cedar chips on top of the ground fence. Coming home that night, Leiney was gone, again. When she finally came home, she had scratches all over her nose and shoulders. She had dug a tunnel and wedged her nose and body in-between the cage and the ground-covered fences, cutting herself. True to her breed, she wanted to roam and run.

She also found a way to open the inside front door of the house to escape. Pete would spend hours driving or walking around looking for her. One time, I asked this bachelor why he bothered with such a dog. He smiled and told me that his many girlfriends love a guy with a dog. He said it showed compassion and besides, Leiney was a faithful companion with a good heart. I liked the "chick magnet" part better. Despite Pete's story, I still was blinded to the need for a dog.

Pete is our only single neighbor on the block. He is a tall, good-looking guy with just enough streaks of grey hair to make him seem responsible to the ladies. He would walk the neighborhood with a new girlfriend (built like a swimsuit model) and with Leiney in the lead. My daughters and I would come to greet them as they passed. As the girls petted Leiney, Pete, with girlfriend in arm, would remark, "Isn't Leiney a good dog!?" He would then wink at me and I would smile, thinking maybe I do need a dog!

Pete told me the story of how he had just set the stage for a romantic evening with his girlfriend. Candles were lit, the fireplace roared, and the wine twirled the senses. Just before the romance began, Leiney returned from the park next door and was scratching at the door. Getting up, Pete let her in. Returning to his warm spot in front of the fire, he again held his girlfriend in his arms. Lips met, the fire roared. Leiney, over the next minute and a half, right in front of them, coughed up a whole package of hot dogs, including the plastic wrapper. Talk about a mood killer. Apparently she stole them from a picnic table during her evening wander.

Leiney wasn't the first yellow Lab to escape and wander the neighborhood, however. Leiney's neighbor and mentor was a Golden Retriever named Rebbie. Her owners told me that she came from six generations of champion royalty (and great tennis ball chasers) from Reddington, Connecticut. Rebbie taught Leiney all that she knew. Rebbie would escape from his kennel and get a ride back to his home by the Delafield Police, too. There he was most days, sitting in the back of the cruiser looking out the window. Rebbie had to be bribed into the police cruiser. The kind officers would give Rebbie doggie treats. Heidi and Howie, Rebbie's owners, told me that they thought Rebbie escaped so that he could get treats from Delafield's men in blue. All this time Leiney watched in the wings and waited for her chance to follow in Rebbie's footsteps. Soon enough she would finally make her break to spice up our sleepy town and get some dog treats.

What a great life for a dog, being chauffeured around the neighborhood while the other dogs watched in envy. I started to think maybe these dogs know what they are doing.

One evening, however, Leiney didn't come home. The next day Pete and his girlfriend drove around looking for her. She'd simply disappeared. Frantically, the Delafield Police were notified.

Delafield is a small town of four thousand people with little or no crime. The police need to have something to do. After twenty years on the police force, the most interesting story told by a retiring police officer: he wrestled a deer out of someone's swimming pool after it had fallen in and after an hour, was about to drown. I know this sounds like something out of "Andy of Mayberry".

This time, unlike Rebbie, there would be no riding home in a Delafield Police car. Leiney was not to be found. Someone had spotted her being dragged into a car by two people in the park where she normally roamed. When Pete got the news, he was heartbroken. His girlfriend cried for days.

After a few months passed, the Humane Society called: "Is this Pete and did you lose a yellow Labrador dog a while back?" They had a found a yellow Labrador in the Delafield vicinity.

Pete almost dropped the phone. He told them he would rush right down and check this dog out. Arriving with his girl-friend, the dog was brought out. This Labrador looked a little lighter yellow in color and was missing some telltale mark-ings.

A huge smile formed on Pete's girlfriend's face as she shouted, "LEINEY!" Tears flowed down her cheeks.

Not one to ruin the moment, Pete simply said, "Welcome home, Leiney!" In his heart he knew he really had a 'Leiney number two'. They went back home, hugged Leiney, and lit a fire in the fireplace. The good old days were back.

After each brief visit with our daughters, Leiney had to go to pursue other neighborhood explorations. Each encounter raised the volume of Stacy's demands for a yellow Lab dog. Soon our friends and neighbors, Dave and his wife Eddi, would bring home a yellow Lab puppy named Dune. Our first mistake was letting that puppy, with paws the size of an adult fist, roam around our house for the girls to see. What was going on in our heads? These girls of ours had high emo-tional quotients, and we just stoked the fires!

Every time the girls saw a dog on television, in the paper or on the street, the louder their demands became for a dog.

One weekend Pete was going out of town, and he asked if we could watch Leiney for two days. I couldn't say no. I reasoned that once the girls had to shovel some poop or see how much responsibility caring for a dog would be, they would end this dog search. Wrong again!

"Sure they are fun to pet, but you have to feed them and keep your stuff from being ruined by their constant appetite for putting things in their mouths," I would remind the girls. With the gusto of Columbus discovering America, I proudly announced, "And they poop and someone has to pick it up!"

Unfortunately, my poop speech had no affect whatsoever on my girls.

Leiney came with a cage, which we brought in and placed in the laundry room. She was a good dog and played with the girls. Stacy and her younger sister, Kari, took turns taking her for a walk. Kari was our happy-go-lucky kid, always smiling and easily brought into any conspiracy, such as putting pressure on Mom and Dad for a dog. At night, we put Leiney in her cage and went to bed. Leiney did not like cages or kennels. She whined, scratched and made enough racket that we had to let her out in order to get any sleep. Maybe this experience would change the girls' minds regarding a permanent family member of the canine variety. These girls were troopers. Stacy and Kari took turns petting her as she slept on the floor in the family room. During the day she would sit on the couch and watch television by herself. Other times, my wife of twenty years, Mary Kay, found Leiney sitting in our family room whining and staring at nothing in particular. Leiney must have missed Pete. This brought back my childhood memories of Patches. I began to remember that these animals have a memory and a heart. They are more than food digesting machines that dirty everything around them. Leiney had a personality and true feelings.

These observations brought about a new understanding. I began to finally listen to the voices of my children and see the reasons behind their longing for a dog. As an adult with great responsibilities, I forgot what it means to be a kid. Dogs are great reminders that comedy and *mischief* should rule your life.

CHAPTER 2:

Dog

Heaven

Substitute Dog

It seemed that everyone around us was getting a Labrador puppy. The new neighbors moved in across the street and out of their car bound a huge yellow Lab named Jake. Their neighbors to the north then decided to buy a yellow Lab and they named him Barney. I tried to ignore the fact that everything in nature seemed to be fighting against me.

My daughters were going nuts each day, bringing more tears and notes, begging for a dog. Pictures of dogs were placed on the car steering wheel or under my pillow. How does a man, with warm blood pumping through his veins, deny the tears of a ten-year-old asking daily for a dog.

With a big smile, Stacy, would ask, "Dad, can we please get a dog? I'll take care of it, give it lots of love, and do everything for it, I promise! *I am a good kid you know!*"

I would respond with a cold 'no', explaining that someday they would be teenagers and Mom would end up caring for the dog. Besides, a dog would dirty things up. We had finally reached that stage where the house had new furniture and carpeting, and it would be very hard to see a dog destroy these things.

What came next was worth an Academy Award given for 'Emotional Rejection' by a child: tears would begin to flow. Not just one or two down the cheek, but a sobbing, sorrowful cry that continued with a crescendo, "I guess (sniff), I will never be a happy child!" Shirley Temple would be proud of this performance.

This, of course, brought out some sneering and laughing by the two older siblings, Peter and Sarah. Kari and Stacy would scream at them to "just shut up," and we were off to the fights. A scenario of such intensity, repeated several times over the months, required the strength of the biblical Job, or at least some spiritual help for Mom and Dad. After much discussion and thought, Mary Kay and I created a plan.

First things first. We decided to see how they took care of a smaller animal, like a fish. How about a fish? They are a part of the animal kingdom, right? Grudgingly, the girls decided to give it a try. Off to the fish store! Sure it is no dog, but fish are much easier to care for than a dog, and much cheaper. Or so I thought. At the fish store, Kari found a tank filled with multicolored fish. They were the kind you see in some doctor's office- big beautiful fish with colorful stripes and lots of castles and shrubbery. The only problem was those fish needed a salt water tank, which required monitoring the salt content, acid content, potassium levels, etc. It seemed like too much trouble unless you were a nurse who worked in the intensive care unit in some hospital and were used to such complicated procedures. Those tanks even came with a MANUAL! I just knew that within one week, all of those colorful fish would be floating at the top of the tank, bloated, because we forgot to put the right amount of salt and pepper into the tank. I just wanted to fill the bowl with a garden hose and be done with it. My plan was to continue to distract my kids with 'substitute animals' until they found some video game or some boyfriend to distract them. After all, I had seven years of college. The battle of the wits, although outnumbered four to one, would be won by me.

"How about this nice orange goldfish?" I questioned. I had a goldfish as a child. I won it at the Wisconsin State Fair ping-pong ball throwing contest in the 1960's. There are always games at these carnivals for the average-Joe trying to win something for his girlfriend or family member. You could win a big stuffed animal if you could get a softball to land in a tipped bushel basket. The "carney" guy would throw the ball over his shoulder and land it in the basket. Not bad, I thought, for a guy with half his teeth missing and a tattoo with "Mom" spelled wrong. So, of course I tried it and found that those soft balls bounced out of those baskets with greater force than I initially used to toss them.

"What is there, some midget behind the basket punching it so the ball doesn't stay?" I inquired.

The 'carney' guy smirked just enough to have his cigarette fall out of his mouth. I looked for an easier game.

I found it in the 'GOLD FISH TOSS'. For a dollar, you were given three ping-pong balls that you throw at about fifty bowls butted up against each other with a tiny goldfish in each one. Unless you ate the ping-pong balls, or threw them into the crowd behind you, you were guaranteed to land it in one of the bowls and be able to take home a goldfish in a plastic bag. One goldfish per three balls. They probably paid a penny apiece for those fish and made a dollar on each kid who tried to win. Not a bad return-100 times on your money. Of course, this was the time before big mutual fund returns, but I am digressing. I won and went home with my goldfish in a small plastic bag feeling proud. My dad put his newspaper down for a millisecond, looked at his nine-year-old son and the goldfish, smiled, and continued smoking his cigar and reading his newspaper. My mom reminded me that fish carried diseases and I should wash my hands if I touched the water. Then she mentioned something about how two-thirds of Europe died of the Plague because some kid did not wash his hands after handling a fish he had won at a Renaissance Fair. It didn't matter, because I actually *won* something at the State Fair. The fish, however, would die the next day. End of story.

"Dad, that's a dumb story," Sarah smirked.

Rolling their collective eyes, the girls brought the attention back to the task at hand and agreed to try out the goldfish to show how responsible they would be.

We finally had a family agreement! Plus, the goldfish are only $4.95 each; I'll take ten! I was still getting the deal of the century!

I reminded the storekeeper that I had won a goldfish twenty-five years ago for a dollar. We Armenians always tell some historical family story to strangers who could care less, but that never stops us. We either enjoy forcing people to pay attention or we enjoy exercising that part of our mind. Whether they listen is immaterial. He just shook his head and laughed.

What was the clerk hiding behind his laugh? Soon I would discover that buying fish was a real money shakedown. A city loan shark would be put to shame. First, we needed the tank, reasonable enough, plus an aerator, because fish need to breath. Second, we needed real and artificial vegetation, so the fish had places to hide and play. Don't forget the stone castle, various rocks, and fake water slide. Who builds a castle underwater and why would fish want to hang out there? Oh, yes, another filter and a special fish that ate the green algae that formed on the glass, without which we wouldn't be able to see the fish. Special cleaning instruments, chemicals, and a video on how to keep your fish happy. Total cost: $225! All for a $4.95 gold fish. Maybe a dog wouldn't be so bad.

The fish died rather quickly, as I predicted, one by one. Each time, I would make a joke about calling in the Flight for Life helicopter the next time a fish got sick. To the kids' credit, they took care of the fish, with feeding and the weekly tank cleaning. But, fish have their limitations. You can't teach them tricks, they don't bark or communicate, or repeat hand or gill signals. They just swim around and after a while, die. No one knows why, and we can't afford an autopsy. I have a theory that fish just get bored to death and expire.

The drumbeat for a dog began to sound. We needed another animal fast.

Mary Kay and I decided to go one step higher than a fish and bought a guinea pig. A guinea pig looks like a chipmunk with a gland condition. They can be described as a huge, hairy baked potato with a head. Ours was light brown with soft fur. The girls gave him the name Peanut. This animal would do three things: eat, sleep, and hump on any object that came near it. Our youngest daughter, Kari, called it "hunching."

"Look, Mom, Peanut is hunching again," she would exclaim.

She told her first grade teacher, and anyone else who would listen, about Peanut and his "hunching" abilities.

Peanut kept the kids entertained, squeaking and hiding under the shredded newspaper, and yes, more hunching. This thing was also indestructible. The kids would drop him accidentally from the top of the ping-pong table and he would continue to function: eat, sleep, and hunch.

Peanut could not fetch a stick or roll over. My son, Peter, and his sisters, soon tired of Peanut. They caught on to the substitute animal routine and were simply tired of this furball with a gland condition. Enter Gail, our friend. She lived alone and loved to hold Peanut. You guessed it. Peanut got a new home and the notes and pleading letters for a dog began to appear again.

When in doubt, take it to the spiritual authorities. Each Sunday during Sunday School, Stacy and her younger sister, Kari, had a prayer request: that God would send them a dog. Now Mary Kay and I were in for Biblical challenges. One Sunday morning Stacy came home with a note from her Sunday School teacher that read, "Dear Dr. and Mrs. Hajinian, I want you to know that our class is praying that Stacy will be able to get a dog."

Our arms were too short to box with God. My mind would wrestle with the thought, "would the family show responsibility in caring for a dog or would it be discarded like a two-week-old Christmas present?" My deep thoughts were immaterial, my wife was the first to give in. I, however, kept looking at the clean carpets and furniture. All this selfishly weighed heavily and I wasn't sure if I could give them up. You see, I grew up in an Armenian-American household where cleanliness was godliness. If you didn't go to church or read your Bible, that was okay, as long as you washed the kitchen floor twice a week. You could be an ax murderer, but if there was no dust on your refrigerator or dust bunnies (balls of dust that are so big they look like animals) under your bed, you were okay. My mom would weekly move the sofa and vacuum under it. We called that Armenian aerobics. My aunt would come by to check the top of the refrigerator for dust. I think in the old country they may have had dirt floors in the villages of my ancestors, but they were *clean* dirt floors.

I couldn't get too excited about dust. What's the big deal? It shows the sunlight filtering through the windows. You can write messages to people on their dining room tables without using a pencil. Then I discovered the gross revelation from my American-Armenian relatives: dust is really dried skin cells. From humans? How did they come up with that? Aren't cells only seen with a microscope? What happens if you get a dog? Would their dead cells form dust? The relatives' answer: Dogs are not clean animals. They don't wipe their feet or use toilet paper. Case closed. My mind was in turmoil again.

Sometimes you make decisions that you know are right for you and your family, but deep down inside you feel that you are betraying some family history or some dead relative is putting the "L" (Loser) sign to his dead forehead. What happens when a person holds two contradictory thoughts in his head for a long time? Does dementia set in? Is there a constant ringing in your ears? You have a gnawing suspicion, but you go through with it anyway. You finally push one thought away and make the other thought justified. I cleared my mind and took a risk.

CHAPTER 3:

The Yellow Labrador Puppy

Puppy Christmas

Like I said, as a child, I had a beagle, the all American dog. Long after I left home and had kids of my own, my dad would tell my kids that the happiest day in his life was when that dog went to doggy heaven. The old dog made a mess after I left home, but still, the best day of his life?

Come on, Dad, I thought, *what about marrying Mom, the honeymoon, my birth, or my sister's, or getting out of the service after World War II? Weren't those the happiest days of your life?*

Maybe those words kept me from getting a dog. It was too late to figure out what Dad had meant by that statement.

Finally, against better judgment, I said, "Okay."

Many times the word "okay" changes your life, for example when you get married, get into your favorite college, or kiss your first girlfriend or boyfriend. In fairness to my children, they were very responsible with the substitute animals. They kept the fish tank clean and kept Peanut, the guinea pig, entertained and fed. Hey, what dad would not want to be a hero to his kids and get them a dog? Little did we know that life would take a sweet turn and for seven short years our whole neighborhood would soon experience a remarkable transformation, all because I said "okay" to getting a dog.

Mary Kay would begin the dog search by talking to friends. My only request was that the dog would be big enough to play and wrestle with. High-strung, foo-foo purse dogs were not my choice, and since I was footing the bill, I had a vote.

There are probably as many breeds and combinations of dog species as there are juice combinations. I remember long ago they used to make simple cranberry juice. Wisconsin is a great cranberry producing state. Just crushed cranberries, a little sugar and viola, cranberry cocktail. That was it. Now they have blended cranberries with apple: cranapple, crangrape, cranrasperry, etc. If those producers could blend it with vegetables or meat and sell it, I think they would. How about cranporkchop or cranchili? Think of the time you would save. No fancy meal preparation or picking up the fork to eat. Just do it all at once. Cranchili for lunch in a convenient bottle.

When I grew up, dogs were either a mutt or a purebred. Now they mix a Labrador and a poodle and get a Labradoodle or a pug and a beagle and get a Puggle. If you mix a Labradoodle, and a Puggle you get something that isn't even mentioned in the Bible. The list goes on and on. Of course, there is always the plain mutt, with no pedigree or claim to fame or worth.

Those mutts make up the majority of loved dogs out there and throughout the history of dogs. Having experienced the friendliness and gentleness of a Labrador, that became our choice. Even President Clinton had a Labrador. The first black Lab to occupy the White House. If it was good enough for the White House, it was good enough for us. After all, seeing President Lyndon Johnson in 1965 lift his beagle puppies by the ears, my parents decided that a beagle would be a good dog for me. Call it a presidential tradition.

So, my family agreed upon the Labrador breed. I soon discovered the Labrador breed is the number one most popular breed in America. It is the Champion of Dogdom. This is a family friendly dog which weighs from 70 to 90 pounds and loves to retrieve things.

The story is told that the breed originated in Labrador, Canada, which is somewhere near Newfoundland. There also seems to be a branch of the family which originated in England. They come in beautiful shades of white, yellow, chocolate brown and shiny black. Since all of the Labs we experienced were yellow, that was the color Mary Kay and the girls chose.

Next, she searched the internet for information about male versus females, small Labs verses large sized. Narrowing it down to a female yellow Lab, she began searching the classified ads in local newspapers. Mary Kay interviewed breeders by phone. Finding a knowledgeable breeder on the phone, she made her decision and decided it was worth the hour and a half drive to Ripon, Wisconsin.

Ripon is a small, sleepy town known for an amazing historical event which literally shaped the United States for the past one hundred and fifty years. This statement would, of course, be debated by Democrats. Ripon, Wisconsin is the official birthplace of the Republican Party! The drive to Ripon is pure Wisconsin scenery. Rolling farms, cows and corn. About ten thousand years ago, glaciers covered the area and, as they melted, small lakes and depressions called kettles were created. These small depressions along the roadside were usually filled with water, which reflects the blue sky dotted by white billowy Wisconsin clouds. I say "Wisconsin sky" because there is truly nothing more beautiful than a summer Wisconsin sky. Okay, I have never been to Oregon or New Mexico. There probably are other awe-inspiring skies in the United States, but not in France. So there.

Traveling along this scene with the emerald green grass and pockets of blue water, reminded Mary Kay and the girls of the reason we live in Wisconsin. This uniquely beautiful road brought them to the town of Ripon. The quiet downtown is surrounded by farms which produce the peas and corn canned by the Green Giant vegetable company. It is also the home to a small farm that bred

Labrador puppies. The beauty of the surroundings was intensified by the thought that we were finally going to bring home a real dog! Driving up the farm road, Mary Kay and the girls were welcomed by a huge yellow Lab male with green eyes, circling around the car. Mary Kay kept hitting the brakes, fearful of running the dog over. Kari and Stacy kept shifting from window to window watching this magnificent animal circle around. Later they would discover that this dog was the father of our future dog.

Still he circled, as if to play with the car while Stacy, nose pressed against the glass, shouted, "Mom, look at how huge that dog is." Her heart could not believe what her big eyes were telling her.

The car came to a halt. As they exited, Mary Kay and the girls were greeted by the breeder and the circling yellow Lab. They were led to a puppy playground. The smell of hay, animals and urine permeated the place. Five cute yellow Lab puppies jumped on each other as they rolled and played, oblivious to Stacy and Kari's reaction to the smells and sights before them. Beneath the pile was a timid puppy being pummeled by her siblings. Feeling sorry for her, Stacy reached down and lifted her out. Her four brothers and sisters kept biting and playing with each other, unaware that someone had snatched their sister.

"How about this one?" Stacy asked.

With amazement, Kari petted her tiny head. Up to this point, the girls had only been around large yellow Labrador dogs. "Yes Mom, can we get this one?" a young Kari pleaded.

"She's the one!" Mary Kay announced. The two month search was over. This puppy, with the small ribs poking through her pink and lightly yellow-haired chest, would have a new home. Paying the breeder and getting multiple care instructions, they packed up and left.

Placing the puppy in a cardboard box in the back seat, the girls laughed with joy as she tried to get out. Her soft tongue and floppy ears would brush against their hands as they petted and played with her. The ride home was full of excitement as the new puppy yelped and pawed at the box.

The front door would burst open with Kari and Stacy running in to announce with a shout, "DAD, WE GOT A DOG!"

Well, finally! Glory be! And why not? You've got a dad and mom who care about their daughters' every whim, I thought.

Following behind them was a tiny yellow Lab with a tiny, ever-beating tail. The newest family member proceeded to bite my hand as I placed it near the floor to pet her. A couple of bites on the hand that, literally, will feed her. She also had the distinct smell of a barn burnished into her fur. Soon enough, she would squat and pee on our new family room carpet. She had tagged her territory.

"Oh no, she just peed," Stacy and Kari, laughing out loud, announced.

Our clean, new home would never be the same. It didn't seem to matter; the long and fateful search had finally ended. The family now had a dog. For two or three years, I'd dodged every dog request bullet. The dog won and I lost. I thought about all of those silly notes and tears the girls had shed for a dog. I looked at the bright smiles and wide eyes of my daughters. My heart went out to them. I began to feel regretful for being so resistive all those years. They were very patient and now we had a puppy!

We all felt the excitement and giddiness of the moment. I was getting rather emotional. A lump kind of appeared in my throat, but soon passed as our new dog bit and scratched at my ankles with her sharp claws and baby teeth.

She'd had to wait a long time to come into our quirky American Armenian family; her life with us was just beginning.

CHAPTER 4:

Puppy Times

Queens Court

Hi, I'm back. Was I missed or what? Yes, I was a darling puppy. I don't remember too much of my mom or dad, or brothers and sisters, I just remember being hugged and squeezed a lot. The new place was so quiet and smelled so different. I was the only dog. Garbo says that I sat looking at my reflection in the window, which made me feel better since I thought I was looking at another dog. I doubt that story. Let's get one thing straight: I'm a *smart* yellow Lab. I know a real dog from a reflection. Another thing I remember: in my excitement I peed on Garbo when he first held me up. He wasn't too happy about that! (He was almost ready to take me back). They put a ticking alarm clock in my bed to remind me of my mom's heartbeat. It actually kept me up for days. Even biting the darn thing wouldn't stop it.

"Into the bath tub," I said and smiled. This soft and playful puppy scampered up the walls of the tub as Stacy and Kari rolled on the floor in laughter. Kari decided to name her after the dog in the musical *"Annie"*. It was their favorite video. When young girls get a video that they like, it becomes ingrained into their brains simply because it is watched over and over. I saw "Annie" once, but the songs reverberate through my head to this day simply because the video was played so much. The dog, named Sandy, is the main comfort for a group of orphans and the object of their affection. My hope would be that our Sandy would comfort my once, *dogless* daughters.

Our neighbors down the block, Dave and Eddi, seconded the name Sandy. It went so well with their large, ever growing, yellow Lab named "Dune". Sandy and Dune: SandDune. So, our newly cleaned puppy Sandy would sleep in the large pen, which housed Leiney for a night or two. We placed an alarm clock next to her to imitate her mother's heartbeat. That night was rough for Sandy and the girls. She would cry and whine the whole night through. A puppy's cries are meant to grab attention. They start out with a timid bark. As the oxygen runs out of their small lungs, their cries for help become an ever diminishing, drawn out yelp. Our collective memory shot back to Leiney's cries at night. Our quiet nights would be no more.

The morning came. Kari and Stacy would bound downstairs with the energy of gift opening on Christmas morning. Time to see the new puppy. A dad feels pretty proud when he can create that kind of enthusiasm simply by saying *okay*. Laughter filled the air as the puppy rolled on her back, bit their fingers, and climbed on their arms. This soft, tiny dog was a handful for them. By now, Peter and Sarah had come down the stairs. Squirming to get out of their grip, Sandy ran towards them. Getting on the floor, Peter covered his head as Sandy began to bite his ears, then his fingers. Sarah would roll on the ground laughing as Sandy took a break from attacking Peter and pummeled her.

Sarah was to take control. She had prepared for the dog by going to the library and getting a book on puppy discipline.

She began to give Sandy her first training lesson, "Sandy, no biting."

She would then tap Sandy on the nose with one finger. This only caused Sandy to tighten up her upper lip, expose her teeth, and bite Sarah's finger! Peter, Stacy and Kari, grabbing their stomachs, roared with laughter. Finally, Sarah had met her match.

Sarah had a good heart. Her problem was, she was meant to be a leader. She was meant to be an only child. Since she had an older brother and two younger sisters, she was forced to be captain of her siblings' 'ship'. Mutiny was their response daily. Sarah had to be the 'mom' during the make-believe 'life on the prairie'. Her two younger sisters and cousins had to be the children. Children had to obey their mother, especially when they lived on the prairie. Now a dog named Sandy had to learn the rules of *prairie living* if they all were to survive. There were chores to be done, water fetched. They had to dress properly, according to Sarah. They would wear my wife's old dresses. The neighbors, who observed the drama, would chuckle, not believing that Mary Kay actually wore such a dress in public. Hey, styles change! What's wrong with an aquamarine mermaid's dress with puffy sleeves? They must have worn something like that in the 1840's on the Kansas prairie. At least, according to Sarah.

"You are not the boss of us!" screamed her sisters during one of the many *Prairie Days* fights. Sometimes you must be a leader and face the underlings' wrath. One October during the World Series (I am referring to the Major League Baseball World Series since now they have World Series for skateboarding and one for poker), Reggie Jackson, the famous New York Yankee star, had just hit his third homerun in ONE game. This was an unheard of feat. I don't think even the great Babe Ruth had set that record. Reggie, through his sheer domination of the sport, became the team leader, whether they liked him or not. His talents overcame his unpopular attitude with the fans. The announcer brilliantly summed up his persona with the comment, "Reggie is the Stick that Stirs the Drink!"

I liked that comment. It stuck in my brain and I have used it ever since to describe my oldest daughter, Sarah. We are not drinkers, but you get the drift.

After Sarah put Sandy down, she pulled Pete aside and hatched a plan. Sitting Kari and Stacy down, Peter and Sarah made them sign an agreement. Knowing that the younger siblings were desperate for a dog, the older siblings made it clear on paper that they would not be responsible for any chores involving the dog. No walking, feeding, cleaning the 'yard business', or any other job not listed in the contract, but which could be invented by Mom and Dad. In the event of their untimely death, they still would not be responsible for any care, concerns, or unlisted items involving Sandy. An untouchable contract. A contract a lawyer would be proud of and could have learned something from. Nonetheless, Stacy and Kari gladly signed it.

Slowly, Sandy began to melt Sarah's heart. She would always sleep by Sarah and rest her head on her lap, even though Sarah did not seek her out. Sandy was the kind of dog that would seek those who were indifferent to her. She had to make them fans. This was a characteristic of Sandy that would reach fruition later in her life.

"Mom, she is so cute," Sarah said, smiling with her orthodontic work beaming. "Don't worry about taking care of her, we have it all worked out."

Stacy took to Sandy with the greatest satisfaction. Stacy, in particular, had something to prove. Three years earlier, she was asked to let out a tan and white Springer spaniel, *Sparks*, for a family while they were on vacation. Stacy didn't know that, due to cancer, the dog would have a short time to live.

Three times a day that poor dog was let out and taken for a walk whether it wanted to or not. Stacy would check her watch every few minutes to see if it was time for her to take the dog for his walk. Finally, the moment would arrive. Like a storm trooper, Stacy would put   on her coat and snow boots, grab the leash and head over to the neighbor's house. We would stand in the window and watch her pull the half-sleeping dog, encouraging him, "Come on, boy."

The dog would walk ten feet and just sit down. "Come on boy, you can do it," Stacy would shout with a big smile on her face and heart.

The next day after the family came back, the dog died. Sarah and Peter kept teasing Stacy by telling her she was responsible. She simply walked the dog to death. This was quite a burden for a five-year-old to carry. We still get a chuckle out of it at Stacy's expense. Now, Sandy would be her showpiece. The world would see, she can love and care for a dog and it won't die the next day.

Sandy slept for the first two days simply due to the changes and exhaustion.

"She's awake!" Stacy would shout.

Kari and Stacy would bound down the stairs and throw the ball at her or force toys in her mouth so she would play. All Sandy would do was bite at the girls and just lay there. The girls would sit by her bed, waiting for signs of playfulness.

Having brought four babies home from the hospital, Mary Kay had some idea of how your life changes when someone new is around! The kids were helpful, but it was Mary Kay who doled out the food and water for Sandy. Mary Kay followed the puppy around the house when television distracted our daughters.

"She's just like a newborn," Mary Kay would assure us.

Sandy was quite different; babies sleep. This dog was on a tear after the first two days of rest. Babies have two legs and crawl; Sandy had four legs which required constant attention. She could be in one room and within seconds, was now upstairs urinating on your bedspread. Babies wear diapers. For Sandy, the floor was her diaper and never in the same room. Her sharp baby teeth would nip your hand or anything that ventured near her mouth. She was ready to bite, tear, chew or lick anything. With her still small paws, she would play and paw at you. When she got upset, she would let out a soft, yet meaningful yelp. The girls loved to tease her just to hear this soft barking. Soon the game became hide and run from Sandy as she would bite your ankles or chew your socks.

Again, babies take naps. Sandy never slept, or if she rested, the slightest commotion would set this soft yellow furball into motion. Still pictures of puppies sell everything. The reason is simply that they are so cute. Even a guy can admit that. Sandy was right up there with the rest of the puppy models.

How do you keep a puppy from destroying everything while her teeth come in? Our neighbors, Dave and Eddi, used a spray called "Bitter Apple", which they spritzed on everything their dog might have chewed on. It had a sour apple smell and seemed to work. Sandy stayed away from the pillows, carpets, shoes, draperies and furniture. People would visit us and remark about the 'apple' smell throughout the house.

"That's Chuck's new cologne," Mary Kay would comment with a straight face.

Sandy would soon discover that the kitchen chair legs were made of oak and were perfect for teething.

"Hey, who's biting these chair legs?" I shouted.

This puppy looked around waiting for someone to come to her defense. It didn't take long before Stacy chimed in, "Dad, it's not her fault. Is it, Sandy?"

Sandy snarls her puppy whiskers up, scuttles over to Stacy and Kari, and starts to chew on their shirtsleeves. Slobbering and wet sleeves would be the norm. Finally, we called our new vet, Dr. Osgood, about Sandy's chewing habits. She reassured us that this would eventually stop. Her baby teeth would soon come out. She proceeded to tell the story about how one of her dogs chewed a number of holes in her leather couch while she was in the kitchen for twelve minutes. Her suggestion? You guessed it: *Bitter Apple spray.*

After about four bottles of Bitter Apple spray, Sandy lost her baby teeth and graduated to rawhide chew sticks. They were meant to last a week, but were gone in a day.

It takes concentration to chew on some dead animal's hide that has been cured and rolled into a cigar shape. Drool and saliva-soaked rawhide covered my oriental carpets. My Armenian thoughts reminded me that saliva is filled with germs. Now my oriental carpets were spotted with dog germs. All I could do was sigh and watch this little dog enjoy her chewing. For most dogs, including Sandy, time stands still until this chew stick is completely gone. There is a job to do: unravel and chew this rawhide, rolled cigar until it has been softened enough to be chewed and swallowed. It involves lots of saliva, chewing, pulling, more saliva and some tearing.

Please don't interrupt me while I am chewing on my rawhide bone. House on fire? So what? I am *masticating*. I love turning a five-inch raw hide bone into a slobbering mess of soft Jello. That job takes concentration. It's not done until it is swallowed and my paws are licked clean. *A boat floats; dogs eat.* **That's our main reason for living. I chewed anything, because everything has a chicken taste. Mary Kay called Dr. Osgood many times about my eating habits. More on that later.**

A heartfelt burp, or paint peeling gas, would follow the end of the bacon-flavored chew sticks.

"Please avoid buying the bacon chew sticks," Peter would beg as he covered his nose and ran through the room.

Peter would bravely grab the end of the chew stick and tug the piece while Sandy held on and growled. As the intensity of the tug-of-war grew, Sandy's growling got louder. As an added measure of intimidation, her upper lip would raise showing all of her teeth. If fear didn't get Peter to let go, she used her final tactic: With the speed and slight of hand of a magician, she would let go of the chew stick, bite Peter's hand, and then grab onto the chew stick again. Depending upon how hard she would bite, Peter would determine whether the chew stick would be released to Sandy's control.

As the months passed, our puppy grew up quickly. Like a newborn, they never return to that helpless state.

I discovered the great outdoors for a bathroom. It certainly was much easier then getting yelled at for going potty inside. Outside had a better view. Still, the inside was warmer, which is important for bathroom activities.

Sandy would begin to exercise her right to manipulate her owners to get what she wanted. She was about to discover her reason for existence. After her first year, the *terrible two's* were soon coming upon us.

CHAPTER 5:

Sandy Discovers the Neighborhood

Four amigos and the explorer

Labrador dogs like me, are driven by our instinct to explore and run away. This need arises in the depths of our hearts and will never be understood by man. We simply honor our inner canine and, here's the fun part, take off for adventure and sometimes, romance! Of course, those took a back seat to finding food at the neighbors'.

Sandy's first interaction with the neighborhood was with Dune, the male yellow Lab who belonged to Dave and Eddi, and was now going on 50 pounds at nine months. They were our close friends who lived on a busy street one block away. Eddi grew up on a farm and was surrounded by animals her whole life. She spoke about raising baby raccoons in her house as a child, as well as tending other farm animals. Dune was their biggest animal without a saddle. At one hundred and twenty pounds, Dune was huge, even by Labrador standards.

Sandy had no fear of this dog, even though she was dwarfed by him. She pestered Dune, running around and nipping at his paws and tail until his indifference faded. He pawed back at her and growled. Immediately, Eddi yelled at Dune, and Sandy rolled over on her back. "Sorry Dune," she seemed to whimper. After sniffing each other, the two parted.

Trying to catch up with Dune, Sandy began to grow, eating bowls of food until her pink stomach was so stretched it seemed ready to burst. The first thing that grows are the paws. Her large yellow paws on those skinny legs just looked simply out of proportion and certainly out of place. This made her gangly. Sandy initially found it hard to control her movements. Soon, her legs would strengthen and strong muscles began to show. She loved to go for walks and the girls made sure she got plenty of exercise. What they didn't know was that Sandy was secretly analyzing the neighborhood. Her mind and instincts were whirling with possibilities. She would pause and look with those brown-green eyes. No amount of calling could bring her out of that trance.

Hey! I had questions. I wanted to know who lived there. Who was doing the barking? Who was that nice lady who drove the van up and down the street five times a day? Yeah, I had questions.

Soon, to our chagrin, she would begin looking for those answers.

The old pink collar was soon replaced by a much larger blue collar, as Sandy's head and body began to catch up with her oversize feet. She stopped her nipping and biting, and began to lick anyone who would give her a pet on the head and eye contact. Licks would be followed by a treat from the old cookie jar. Our three-level home became her universe.

Labrador dogs have such a keen sense of smell that they are used as arson sniffing dogs. They can detect accelerants that help determine whether a fire was accidental or incendiary (arson). This great sense of smell led Sandy to great explorations.

Her gifted sense of smell would lead her to investigate hidden treasure chests and bedroom closets. This same sense would cause her to bark and cry until we moved the couch so she could get the remnant "Cheeto". After all that hard work, she would treat herself to the ever famous, Champagne drink from the toilet. Rather than spending our time searching for her, we discovered a sure-fire 'dog bell'. That rattle of the clay lid on the dog treat cookie jar would bring her to attention. Immediately, she would come running from upstairs or the basement. Dog treats were to be had!

Labrador dogs need something in their mouths constantly, and they like to play rough when allowed. Sandy played true to her breed. My son Peter found a new friend in Sandy. Living with younger sisters can be very trying.

Peter had found a companion to run around the yard with. Although she was still a girl, Sandy would play just like a guy. As Pete would sled down the hill, Sandy would beat him down and then jump on the moving sled to knock him off. Once she disabled him, she would pull his hat off and drag it through the snow. This was Sandy's way of playing fetch. You, the human, had to retrieve the object from *her* mouth. It may be your hat, one of your shoes, your purse, really any object you needed immediately. She wanted to be chased. Knowing that you could never catch her, she would bring the object within inches of your hand, teasing you. Any quick hand movements were futile. She was gone. Resting safely ten feet away, she would wag her tail and growl at you with the object in her mouth. She liked to tease the weak human.

Finally, after ten minutes, as a goodwill gesture, she would release the object at your feet. Whatever was released simply could not be worn. It was soaked with her saliva. You usually never got the object back until she was tired of chewing it, you bribed her with a treat, or the door bell rag. When the door bell rang, Sandy would race to the front entrance and welcome the guests in with the object held hostage. Bras and underwear were only released in front of guests.

CHAPTER 6:

Training and Restraining: Dope on a Rope School

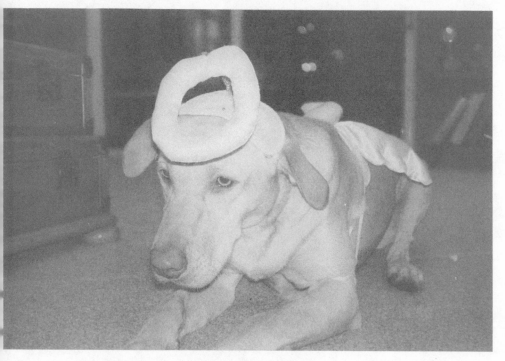

Angel Dropout

As she grew older, Sandy began to wander. Not too far at first. Then, each neighbors' yard became a stepping-stone to go a little further. Eventually, we were walking the street looking and calling for that dog. Sandy could have been the dog in the movie "*Mission Impossible*", except there was no dog in that movie. She would come outside with you right at your side. She gained your confidence. Slowly, she would allow space to develop between the two of you. Labs, with their cunning eyesight, can locate the *blind spot* angle of their master's eyeball. Sandy used this characteristic to her advantage. For one split moment you would take your eye off of her to open the mailbox and boom, she was gone. Always muffled, always discreet. You would take the mail back into the house and realize that the dog was not following you. You might even forget she was with you. Silently gone.

We soon discovered the dangers of roaming. Dave and Eddi showed up one day with tears in their eyes. They had just suffered the loss of their 120-pound yellow Lab, Dune. It seems that Dune had climbed a five-foot fence and ventured out on the busy road that joins the road we live on. A car had hit Dune and they found him in the driveway. I hugged my buddy. My friend Dave is a surgeon and has saved many lives. He has also seen patients die (not because of his work, though). Tears continued to flow down his cheeks as he told us what had happened. I gave him a hug but thought, a grown man cry-ing? *Come on, these dogs live like kings.*

Sandy had not grown on me yet. Right now she was an ornery dog who didn't follow orders. Within two weeks, Dave and Eddi would have purchased a chocolate Lab named Cazador, and ordered a new yellow Lab already named Dune. There seemed to be a gnaw-ing hole in their hearts that needed to be filled.

We began to worry about Sandy. She would bolt here and there, chase cars, circling them until they surrendered their occupants. Once they got out, she would jump on them, banging her paws into their chest, gut or groin. This got their visual attention. She pro-ceeded to lick their faces and roll on her back for a belly scratch. Her pretty green eyes melted the hardest heart. However, not everyone was thrilled with this nuisance of a dog. Many times we would be yelling to deaf ears: "Sandy, come home now! This time we mean it! Come home!"

Mary Kay would go driving up and down the street, sticking her head out the window, looking for a yellow flash of lightening dash-ing from yard to yard. Sandy would then stand perfectly still hoping not to be seen in the neighbor's yard. Finally, unable to control her emotions, Sandy would bolt towards some neighbor taking groceries into her house. The neighbor would be forced to put her grocery bags down and pet this dog of ours. We didn't know who these people were. *Our neighbors are busy*, I thought. Kids have hockey, soccer, singing lessons or sailing, and moms are even busier. As time went on, it seemed the neighbors didn't mind the intrusion. Sandy made them not just slow down, but set the stress aside and stop for that moment.

Who could resist me, a soft, yellow bundle rolling on her side, tail wagging, just begging to be petted? I loved visiting the neighbors, that was great. But, I couldn't understand why all

those neighbors lived by themselves. Why didn't they just live with us, the Hajinians, in one big kennel?

A one-acre yard is only the beginning. If our neighbor was raking leaves, Sandy would be over there, rolling on her back, showing off her brown spotted belly in a submissive move. Of course, our neighbor John would put down his rake and pet her. Any time a neighbor had a project in the yard or garage, Sandy would find a way to get there.

I have been to Texas and Arizona during the fall months, but nothing compares to a Wisconsin fall. People travel from all over the United States to see the beautiful leaf colors and smell the crisp chill of Wisconsin air. The giant oaks with their full canopy of color, some eight feet in diameter, over two hundred years old; the beautiful Catalpa trees with their large, olive-green, spade-shaped leaves contrasted by the long, brown, seed pods; and the red maples, all begin to drop their vibrant leaves. The wind whips them from yard to yard until all the neighbors have an equal amount of leaves to rake and burn. The naked trees exposed Sandy's adventures throughout the neighborhood, but that didn't stop her from wandering. She continued exploring the neighborhood yards, garages, driveways, acting as if her owners were completely oblivious to her whereabouts. The neighbors got used to seeing her and went about their business of yard work or garden planting while Sandy sat and watched.

On one fall day, I found a pair of leather work gloves on my work bench. I used many kinds of work gloves, but found these gloves extremely comfortable and soft. While I raked my leaves, I started a conversation with John. Soon, I was sharing how comfortable these gloves were. He remarked that they were this expensive brand made from the finest lambs' hides with imported wool lining. They were the Cadillac of work gloves. I told him that I'd found them on my work bench.

As he took a closer look, he remarked, "I had a pair just like those, but I can't seem to find them."

I simply took them off and looked down. Entering the conversation and the space between us was Sandy. She very gently tried to bite the gloves that I was holding.

"I think I can tell you how they got in my garage!" I ashamedly remarked to John as I handed them to him. We both looked down at the Sandy. Her whole body began to wag as her head moved from side to side in the opposite direction.

John just laughed and petted Sandy on the head. "Good girl."

Sandy ignored the compliment and tried to tease the gloves out of John's hands with her front incisors.

I smiled and walked Sandy back, my red, embarrassed face hidden. *Somehow I have to keep this dog home,* I thought.

All of our neighbors and friends, with the exception of Leiney, kept their dogs inside the house, in an outside kennel, or restrained by an electric fence. The last implement is the most interesting. A wire is buried into the ground in the perimeter of the yard about six inches deep. The dog wears what is termed a 'shock collar', which activates and releases a small electric jolt as the dog approaches the wire or yard boundary. Wandering dogs can be dangerous to young children, other animals, uncovered garbage cans, speeding cars and meticulous gardens. The shock collar is meant to warn the dog that he or she is approaching a no-go zone. Some Labrador dogs will take the electric stun and fly through the pain to the adventures of the neighborhood. We had to choose for Sandy. Sandy was also learning to either obey her instincts or listen to a greater authority, kind of like humans.

We would let her out and after she had done her business, she would come to the door and bark or scratch at it. Most of the time, that is. As she got older, she would begin to take her time finding the right spot for bathroom duties. Perhaps this bush, no this pile of leaves or right on the concrete walkway! This, of course, got a little annoying when, for whatever reason, we had to wait for her outside in the middle of winter while she diligently scouted out a better outdoor bathroom location.

If a neighbor pulled into their driveway, she was gone. Once she arrived at their home, she made her announcement by jumping on the neighbors and licking their faces. This was followed by her famous rolling on her back in submission to have her belly scratched. This became quite embarrassing for us to get our dog back home. We would call Sandy and then have to ascertain if the neighbor was bothered, angered, or tickled pink by this crazy dog!

Dave and Eddi saw our dilemma and lent us their hand-held shock collar unit. This collar would fit around the dog's neck and with a hand-held device, you could activate a small or large shock to the dog's neck if she went where she wasn't supposed to, or if she was not following your direction. This system did not require digging up your yard and burying a small wire. Our daughter Stacy would parade Sandy around the yard showing her where the boundaries were. The problem was Sandy did not speak a word of English and had a selective hearing problem.

Off she would go, followed by our yell, "Sandy, stay home." The neighbors began to get a kick out of this family with the uncontrollable dog. Sandy became the neighborhood entertainment. This time we had the upper hand. We continued to shout, "Sandy stay! Home Sandy!" Halfway into the street she would get zapped. This would cause her to yelp and stop in her tracks. Her forward momentum would cause her to slide on her belly when her legs stopped moving. This was repeated several times for our slow learner.

Is there something in the manual on dog physiology that tells you how many times you can zap a dog with a slightly painful electric shock before it becomes abseWe must have come pretty close. After a few days of "Sandy stay", followed by a zap and then two yelps from the helpless dog, Sandy began to lose the hair on her neck. It got to the point that when she saw the hand-held phone-size object, she knew a shock was coming if she didn't heed our call. During one episode, while my mother-in-law, Shirley, was on the phone, Sandy pulled the door handle and pushed the screen door open. Before the door closed, she was gone.

Bounding off the couch, Shirley ran into the driveway and threatened her by waving the portable phone. Sandy was smart, but not smart enough to tell that the portable phone could not really zap her. The real zapper was wedged between the sofa cushions, hidden. She turned around and came home. Through one month of 'yelping' we had to make a decision. Enough was enough; we gave the electric collar back to Dave and Eddi. Sandy's cries bothered us each time. Would you shock your kid? Heavens no! Sandy had become our fifth child.

Sandy was about to become a fixture of the neighborhood. With her waging tail, she would look out for cars, then run and prospect the neighborhood. She'd visit anyone in their yard, chase a few squirrels, tease the other locked up dogs, and wait to be called home. Standing in the driveway for all to see, I would yell, "Sandy, come home!" She would stand frozen a hundred yards away looking right at us. It was the ultimate stare down. My anger would rise as I continued to call her name. *Damn dog,* I thought. She would win the stare down. At times, I would have to go and get her. It was like catching a greased pig.

She thought it was playtime, darting back and forth, and simply rolling on her back with her big paws kicking at my hands as I caught her by the collar. Now *my* life was in danger as an occasional car would make its way down the street. After awhile, I would carry her home as she *rubber-necked* around as the other barking dogs looked through the house windows or yard kennels. Her claws would dig into my arms and if I protested her squirming, she simply licked my face. She would win all the time. At times, I could not catch her. Later, I would give up and walk the half block home only to find her waiting on the porch for me. That dog knew.

I have four kids and know how to motivate them to do just about anything. For Sandy, her weakness was doggy treats. Mary Kay showed me how easy it was to get Sandy to come home. "Treat Sandy! Sandy, treat!" she would yell.

Like a cannon shot, I could hear Sandy's nails on the asphalt road, then a yellow blur and finally her majesty herself jumping up for the doggy treat.

Mary Kay decided that Sandy simply needed dog training. Sandy was enrolled in dog obedience school. Relating the story, Mary Kay confided, "Ten dogs were placed in a circle and each dog would pass another dog and learn to behave and heel. She thought this was great fun, but had a real hard time not wanting to sniff the other dogs and say hello. She had to obey the commands, but struggled to pay attention. When commanded to 'sit, stay or give paw', Sandy would just lick the instructor's hand. Eventually with love and discipline, Sandy learned."

In that environment, we all do. Arriving with a big smile, Mary Kay would proudly tell me what Sandy could do: sit, stay – Sandy did neither! When given her cue, she would scratch herself and sniff around. "Who are these people and what do they want" must have been her thoughts.

"Nice school. What are we paying for this?" I would remark.

"Wait, she did it at the class. SANDY SIT!" Mary Kay would command. She began using hand signals in case the dog was suddenly deaf. Nothing but boredom and tail wagging.

Sandy wanted a treat for that kind of obedience. We slowly came around to that loop: command-treat-performance.

"*Dope on a rope*," I 'knighted' Sandy as I petted her head.

The final week of training was about to begin. Mary Kay followed all of the protocol. Walking Sandy around in a circle, she began with the verbal cues.

"Heel! Stay! Release!"

This time Sandy listened! She sat, she stayed, she would come, heal and "leave it." She did them all and on cue!

The teacher was so excited. "Good SANDY!" she exclaimed.

Treats for everyone; Sandy passed. Standing tall and proud, her tail beat out a fast drumbeat while her head swayed in tempo. Sandy arrived home with a blue ribbon and a small graduation medal on her collar. Not bad for two hundred dollars. If we only had those goldfish. They don't go to obedience school. I could have saved the two hundred dollars and spent the money on golf balls.

Hey, I got a graduation medal. Help me out here. I didn't go to preschool. I left home at two months. At least I am not a dumb dog who chases her tail all afternoon. Talk about dumb. Some dogs failed the class and others got "extra credit help". One bribed the teacher! I was quite proud that I got a blue ribbon, a medal, and a diploma. I faked it on the final exam. What's the big deal – sit, stay and walking in a circle'? What is this the French Foreign Legion?

Just as I had to say okay to getting a dog, I had to say okay to her wandering. It seemed that the neighbors, whom we now were getting to know, began to like Sandy's visits. We had lived here for over eight years and hardly knew anyone. Part of that was our fault. Some of the fault fell on the busy neighbors. It didn't matter. Sandy was changing things. A new celebrity was in town.

At home she put on a show. She would sit, stay and release objects. Later, she would discover that actors get paid. She would only do these 'people invented tricks' for the price of a doggie biscuit. Now, we were proud of our graduate. Kari and Stacy would show her new abilities off to the amazement of the neighborhood kids. The clamor for a dog would begin to reach the parents of those kids. Not wanting to explore the life changes of dog ownership, they began to see Sandy as a substitute dog for their kids. Instead of a nuisance, Sandy was invited to visit these families. The newly crowned *neighborhood dog* was about to receive an offer she couldn't refuse.

An invitation arrived in the mail. Since Sandy passed the Dope on a Rope Obedience School test, she was invited to walk in the Thanksgiving Holiday Parade in Oconomowoc, Wisconsin. This is a town five miles west of Delafield. Oconomowoc means "place of gathering waters" or "home of the white-tailed beaver", whichever white settler's interpretation of the Indian word you wish to believe. The *real* rumor came from the 1840's, when a tired early immigrant settler stopped in the dirt road that made up the city and said, "I con no more walk," thus the name Oconomowoc.

This parade is typical of small town parades, the best the town has to offer. The big red fire truck, a few vintage, convertible cars with the town's beauty queen, and the mayor and other politicians throwing out candy to the crowds. The police had to hold back the kids to keep them from being run over or trampled on as they darted back and forth to pick up the candy scattered all over the parade

59

route. Also completing the parade were local marching bands, and kids with banners like "4-H Club" or "HomeMakers' Society".

Finally, bringing up the rear of the parade, Sandy and other dogs were walking with their owners side-by-side. Each wore a costume. Sandy had an outfit of white angel wings and a silver halo hanging over her head, strapped to her neck. She kept shaking the halo off, which was a sign of things to come.

The crowd roared with laughter as she passed. She was anything but angelic. Again, the crowd pleasing comic. With her worst behavior, she was licking and sniffing everyone in sight. Sandy would pull to the side of the parade and grab a tootsie roll out of the hand of an unsuspecting five-year-old. Tears would stream down the child's face. Sandy kept moving. Stacy and her cousin, Renee, spent their entire time pulling on the leash and pulling unclaimed candy out of her mouth. She was not a happy dog, nipping at their hands as they rescued wrapped candy from her throat.

Hey, the candy was up for grabs. Why were those two gagging me? I was bred for hunting, to pull dead animals out of lakes for hunters, not to be dressed up like a angel with wings and a halo that kept falling off my head. There I was cold, hungry and confused in the middle of a parade with weird looking kids who had metal wires and candy on their teeth, and laughing at *me*! Just give me my candy.

As Thanksgiving passed, Christmas would soon come and with the holiday, presents would abound. Even Sandy got a present: a chew toy that squeaked.

Early Christmas morning, the family would discover that Sandy still could not distinguish the great outdoors from the indoors for potty business. There beside the Christmas tree was her latest bowel movement.

"Dad, it is not her fault. She smells the pine Christmas tree," Stacy reminded us.

"Smart dog. She thinks she is outside," laughed Sarah.

"Next year, we get an artificial tree, if she is not potty trained by then," Mary Kay remarked.

She won't be living here if she isn't potty trained by the end of January, I thought. The gifts were opened. Sandy actually got all of the presents. Actually, she claimed them all. Chewing on slippers, Kari's new pajamas, swallowing Peter's puzzle pieces, the list goes on and on. Like a robot out of control, she found everything to place in her mouth and did not let go. Eventually, she found her chew toy that makes noise with each squeeze. Bad move. "Squeak, squeak squeak, squeak," we heard incessantly. She finally tore the toy apart, and chewed and swallowed the noise mechanism. Finally, we could turn the sound down on the television.

As time went on, Sandy stopped her biting. Actually, she was just teething. Her baby teeth were slowly replaced by adult teeth. Her constant biting was replaced by affectionate licks. She was beginning to feel at home with her new family.

CHAPTER 7:

Spring
on the Water

Teasing Sandy

At two years of age, Sandy would now sit and raise a paw as long as we had a treat in our hand. She still acted as an independent dog though, sitting where she wanted, jumping on unsuspecting visitors, and pushing open any door with her nose. This, of course, led to an escape to the wild frontier of the yard, lake and neighborhood. We thought about sending her back to "dope on a rope" school. She already had a 'degree' from a prominent training school, so what would she get from a 'masters of obedience'? Mary Kay was tired of her whining and slobbering in the car each time she drove there. She would cry in the back seat, then force her way into the front seat and finally wedge her head between Mary Kay and the steering wheel. This would go on for the whole twenty-minute ride, back and forth. Mary Kay would walk through the door, a little shaken, with messed up hair. I'd think, *What the hell happened to her?*

"Sandy learned to 'stay' in dog school," Mary Kay would tell me as she collapsed on the couch.

Mary Kay was not going back, which meant neither was Sandy. We would just have to try our own method of rolling up newspapers and swatting her on the snout. She simply did not speak the Queen's English.

For all of her obedience problems, Sandy was a beautiful Lab dog. Her father had chocolate Lab blood in him and was yellow-coated with green eyes. Her mother, a beautiful yellow Lab, had light-colored, aware, eyes, too.

This made Sandy a "Dudley". She had the most sorrowful green eyes, but her mouth was constantly smiling. At times you felt her sorrow, then it dawned on you that her smile revealed that it was all a trick. You were being hypnotized to give her the human food you were eating or a dog treat.

A year or two would pass and Sandy's body grew to maturity. She began to run and hit her stride. In the movie *Chariots of Fire,* the missionary and future 1906 Olympic champion, Eric Liddle, explains to his doubting sister, that God had made him fast and when he runs, he senses God's pleasure. So it was with Sandy. She was a thing of beauty running with speed and agility over ditches and through bushes. Sandy was grunting and breathing wildly as she raced around at full speed. I sensed an enjoyment on her face as she sped by. God had made her fast. My children, who were now becoming teenagers, got their exercise by chasing her endlessly around the obstacles in the yard. NO ONE CAUGHT SANDY. Her long lean torso stretched out as her large paws dug into our meticulously groomed gardens of bulbs and flowers.

"Who dug up all of these perennials?" Mary Kay's empty words escaped into space. Not only were we fighting assaults on our flowers by deer, wild turkeys and chipmunks, we now were faced with repairing the damage of a thrasher dog.

Watching her chase a tennis ball or retreat from a neighbor's yard was a marvel of dog mechanics. Being low to the ground, she would make sharp curves in her running pattern which would be the envy of any NASCAR driver.

Our favorite time was summer with Sandy. Labs love to chase tennis balls off the end of a pier. I have heard of "retrieve the tennis ball" games lasting three hours with the arm of the thrower finally giving out.

With a 30-foot running start, Sandy would leap into the air, fully stretched, flying close to 15 feet. We called this "big air". A big belly flop splash would be followed by her grabbing the ball. With her tail wagging underwater, her yellow brown fur would slice through the sunlit silver and blue waves. This was our entertainment. Stacy would laugh and throw the ball twenty to thirty times. I would swim alongside Sandy and occasionally grab her pumping shoulders to be dragged along. I had seen dolphins do that, why couldn't my yellow Lab? Swimming was always interesting. While treading water with my head barely above the surface and talking with some friends, Sandy would sneak up and climb up my back. This, of course, hurt as her nails dug in and the surprise attack made you jump. Was this a large fish attacking? She just wanted constant attention.

Each time, Sandy would drop the ball at our feet and find someone who sat on the pier and looked dry. If you didn't pick up the ball and throw it back into the water, a price was to be paid. The next move was to shake every last drop of water off her torso onto the pier and the dry people next to her.

"Sandy!" we'd yell in unison.

In that sunlit summer day, Sandy stood panting and dripping with a snicker on her face. She was having a blast. Life was great!

We Labs love to be in water. With my large lung capacity, I float like a battleship. My paws are my paddles as I glide through the water with a tennis ball stuck in my teeth. I sometimes would carry a four-foot log. Hey, that's what I call living.

When someone is playing ball with me, well, I feel loved. Being lonely is worse than anything. One time they left me alone for a whole day. My mind couldn't handle it. Okay, I admit it. I was so bored, I chewed up the carpet in the family room. Someone must have spilled something sweet on the carpet, because it smelled so good. Once I pulled up a thread, each piece unraveled easily. Boy, did I get in trouble when the family came home. They ended up shifting all of the furniture to cover the six-inch hole I put in the carpet. What a goofy arrangement.

Her sense of smell never failed her when she went outside. Some of her finds were dead animals. Some were fast-moving chipmunks. Sniffing around in the yard, Sandy would catch the scent and sight of a squirrel. The squirrel would freeze five feet from the trunk of the tree and ten feet from Sandy. Squirrels are interesting animals. They have eyes on the sides of their heads and can see forward and sideways at the same time. Sandy would slowly sneak up on the grey squirrel as she thought the squirrel was looking straight ahead and couldn't possibly see her! Boom! Up the tree the squirrel would leap as Sandy raced towards another empty chase. At times, the squirrels would conspire to run in two directions totally frustrating Sandy, as she couldn't decide which one to grab. She's fast, but the squirrel can cut and run its way out of any situation.

Occasionally, ducks would come by and distract her as well. Other animals, except dogs, drew Sandy's wrath. Squirrels, chipmunks, and even wild turkeys were fair game to be barked at, chased and harassed. Chipmunks were fast animals. Sandy never caught one. A group of ducks would quietly swim past the pier, almost effortlessly gliding with the current. Sandy would have none of that. Running wildly, she would jump into the water, startling the calmly swimming aquatic birds with her barks. They would panic, scatter and fly away. Back to the pier she would swim proudly, showing everyone who was boss. After being scolded for chasing the ducks, she would put her head down, and huff and puff.

One afternoon, Mary Kay came up to the house exhausted and quite angry. Being dragged up the steps was a wet Sandy with her tail between her legs. Stacy, Kari and Sarah followed laughing. It seemed that Sandy was chasing ducks, but, instead of flying away, these ducks swam out to the middle of the lake. Sandy simply followed. By the time Mary Kay noticed, Sandy was in the middle of the lake where the water ski boats and jet skis were flying around. She quickly called the girls and went out with the boat to bring her in. All they could see was Sandy's little head bobbing up and down, and her powerful shoulders kicking up the water. Bashing through the waves, they caught up with Sandy. The look on her face was saying, "Hey, what are you guys doing out here?" Commandeering a large boat with jet ski waves pounding the hull is not the easiest thing. Add to that pulling a wet dog up into the boat, and all of this adds a little stress.

What would summer be without Sandy and the lake? She would always be at our sides when we went to the pier. A nice, private romantic moment? Forget it. Sandy would sit and watch the sunset with us. During the day, she would greet the neighbors' boats by jumping after them in the water. All we could think about was this dog being caught between the twirling motor prop and the pier.

Sandy was simply too smart for that. Like the cars in the street, she would dodge danger regularly. Maybe she was just lucky. It got to the point where the neighbors would say hello to Sandy while we just waved. She became the red carpet celebrity. The local *Lake and Country Magazine* put a picture of Sandy on their feature story of *Lake Living*. Apparently, Sandy would sit still for a photographer. Her golden-green eyes won over the cameraman. There she was, sitting between Mary Kay and I, looking regal as she squinted in the bright sunlight. The photo op took one take. Sandy was the consummate professional.

"Finally the obedience school has paid off," Mary Kay proudly pointed out.

Our neighbors had a floating raft where their children and friends played. Sandy would stand 100 feet away on our pier. We knew she wanted to go and try to get on their floating raft. Now it was our turn to tease her.

Collectively, we smugly said, "No Sandy, stay."

She would whine louder and her tail would wag faster. This was, again, our time for fun. "No Sandy, stay," we firmly said. Her cries would be deeper, almost a suffering cry. They would start out low: "Awhhh, oohh, awahhh," then reach a higher and louder pitch.

As Kari would plead for us to let her go, Sandy would become strangely silent as she waited for our reaction to Kari's pleas. Her ears would pin back as she waited for our decision. As the word "okay" left my lips, she was in the air, ready to hit the water, immediately swimming to the raft.

There was only one problem: the raft sat on barrels and was two feet out of the water. The only way onto it was by a ladder.

With her head barely out of the water, this Lab was not to be denied. She climbed up the ladder and climbed onto the raft to the squeals and pets of the neighbor girls. Their black Lab, Reggie, was older and too heavy to make such a move. Sandy gazed at Reggie whose tail wagged as she lay on the shore. Then, her gaze moved our way. After a few short moments, she would leap off the raft, swim back to her home pier, ready for a new adventure.

Yeah, man, I always liked a crowd. I'd swim out to the raft with two families watching. Reggie's family, who owned the raft, had a big party going on. I was part of the entertainment. But the panicking Hajinians kept yelling at me to come back, while those on the raft were cheering me on. I love an audience. I like showing off in front of Reggie. She's so lazy.

CHAPTER 8:

White Sails and Blue Breezes

Start of the Race

Spring was the time of year for my daughters to prepare for summer sailing. Getting the boats out of storage and locating the sails and various equipment filled all the days of the week. For over one hundred years, the sailors on the lake that we live on, Nagawicka Lake, have plied the waters in competitive races using only the wind and their guts for power. My son and daughters would add to that tradition. Like their great, great grandfathers, they were privileged to experience the wind in sails. My wife spent her summers on these glaciers created, inland lakes. Mary Kay's grandmother had run a mini summer camp on Beaver Lake for Mary Kay, her eight siblings, and her seven cousins. Lessons of golf, ballroom dancing, swimming, knitting and, of course, sailing, filled their enchanted summers. Sailing was in the family's blood.

Early June was the start of sailing school. Sarah and Stacy were joined by other kids on the lake and some who lived off the lake, but still had a love for sailing. Each summer day included sailing instruction, and twice a week a race would be held. Sarah, being older by three years, would usually win. However, Stacy began to catch on and skipper her own boat. Weeks would pass and Stacy's skills improved to the point of beating her older sister in the Wednesday afternoon and Saturday morning races. With the neighbors, we would follow the race in a boat. Other neighbors would come up to the boat and share some breakfast treats and coffee. This became the communal gatherings for all those parents whose kids were involved in sailing. We would meet in the middle of the lake and eat breakfast while watching the kids battle wind, waves and their competitors. The sailors had great 'abs' and we ate donuts.

Some of the lake people had their well-behaved dogs on their boats. These dogs sat there in the rocking boats. Donuts were left unmolested inches from their mouths. These were well-trained and disciplined dogs, or else they took drugs. Sandy's last trip in the boat became a wrestling match the WWF would have been proud of. She would run from one end to the other and jump on everyone. She would cry and whine as she looked over the water. What did she want? Her bark would tease us with uncertainty as she teetered on the front edge of the boat. Was she going to jump in? The water was cold! How would we get her back in the boat? Would someone have to swim after her? Those questions raced through my head as I raced to grab her collar and keep her in the boat. Seeing dogs in other boats became a major emotional event. Sandy knew the four-legged creature was a dog, but had no idea who it was. The cries and barks were a genetic desire deep in her chromosomes to smell and study every dog on the planet. We forgot what was happening on the racecourse. All eyes were on Sandy. Afterward, she was simply tied to the largest flower pot in the yard until we came back from the race.

Coming to the shore, Stacy would be beaming while her older sister Sarah would huff and puff with an attitude that could be cut with a knife.

"Nice race, Sarah," Mary Kay would retort.

"My younger sister beat me again. This boat sucks," Sarah would snap back. "I was cut off by 'Spam' (a fellow competitor) at the start," she would continue to explain.

Sarah was fun to hug when she was upset. And that is exactly what I would do.

"Sarah, you sailed a fine race. The wind shifted on your last leg up. Otherwise, I think you would have won!" I lied, holding my arm around her shoulder.

"Yeah right," she'd snap as she folded her sail.

Bolting down the stairs from the house would be a wild Sandy. Scampering to jump on the girls, the trouble would start.

"Get off my sails with your sharp nails, you dumb dog," Sarah would yell. "You are such a nuisance. Go away! Go away!"

"Come here, Sandy. Ooh, you are a good dog. Did you miss me? Huh? Give me a lick. Come on, Sandy. Come on," Stacy laughed.

Kari would help tie up the boats while Peter put away the gear. Another beautiful Saturday morning.

Sailing would fill our lives. For over ten years we would sail five times a week. The girls went to sailing school three days a week, races two days a week, and travel to local lakes for regattas. Those were our vacations: sail on our lake, pack up and sail on someone else's lake.

Sandy would spend her afternoons waiting for the sailboats to come back to the shore.

This was very difficult for her.

I don't understand why sailing is so important. Labs do not like to be left alone. I deeply need someone to pet me and give me constant attention. This is why I am a great dog for extraordinarily energetic kids. Usually, I was tied up on a twenty-foot leash to allow me to roam in a limited area. Sleeping in the cool grass,

a squirrel would race by forcing me to jump to my feet and race around until the choke collar pulled me off my feet. I would be driven to sleep by the contrast of the hot summer morning and the cool green grass caressing my belly. Again, the squirrels would make their scratchy noises on the large oak trees. Like an irritating off-key piano, these fuzzy animals would run up and down the tree until I awoke. Repeating the chase up the tree, I would again find that my leash was too short for the chase. Come on! The squirrel would win again. Letting out a big sigh, I would lay my head down again.

While she waited for the returning boats, three large metal flower urns, weighing fifty pounds each, would get knocked over. With the flowers rolling down the hill, Sandy continued to bark at the returning boats. She wanted in on the party. With constant whining and soft barking, she would eventually get her way. Mary Kay would let her off her leash.

Free at last, free at last. Oh finally, I got released!

Letting out a number of loud barks, Sandy bound down the steps, aching to fly into the water. Tail straight into the air, paws outstretched with her eyes squinting, she hit the water. Within a moment's notice, she would swim to our two daughters' boats coming into a buoy to take down their sails. This process was repeated for years.

Hey, that's our swimming instincts. Dogs are dogs. We only think on a certain level. When I sit looking at the sunset, do I have deep thoughts? Heck no! I don't necessarily enjoy staring at the big ball in the sky. It hurts my eyes. I certainly can smell fragrant flowers, but give me the lake. I love to swim!

Basically, I listen to my body and tell my brain what to do: eat, drink, look for fun, and hunt for a place to relieve myself. I

spend lots of time sniffing when it comes to finding a place to "tag". I sniff and scratch the ground, sniff some more, and finally relieve myself on just the right tree or bush.

I usually can tell what kind of animal was here before I arrived. My sense of smell is the finest of the animal kingdom. Come on, at least potty trips are not constantly on my mind like most senior citizens. We don't plan our trips around bathroom breaks. We go when and where we want to. I think Oprah Winfrey calls that *empowerment*!

Sandy and Garbo

CHAPTER 9:

Championship
Sailing

Stacy and Erin

Boy, were there the people on the lake! Everyone seemed pumped at the Hajinian house. Stacy told me about a big race. I rolled on my back and let her rub my tummy for good luck.

It had been twenty-eight years since a young, Nagawicka Lake sailor had won the coveted Wisconsin Yachting Association Championship trophy. As young as five years of age, and all the way to sixteen years old, the sailors on the inland lakes sail a cub or X-boat. It is a two-person, sixteen foot craft with a center board and pointed bow with two sails, a main and a jib. Sailing is gender friendly. Each boat has a skipper who decides on where the boat goes, and the crew, who follows the orders of this mini-captain. Both skipper and crew must be one in motion and mind in order to compete with the other boats. Such skills as reading the wind on the water, pulling in the sails, and hiking over the edge of the boat to balance the wind, are necessary to be competitive.

Stacy was crewing for her brother when she was five. She started skipping a boat when she was ten years old. At the end of the sailing season in early July, ten area lakes would be sending their best sailors to Nagawicka Lake for the Wisconsin Yachting Association Championship. This organization has been holding this championship since 1946 for the X-boats, and since 1938 for the adult boats. It is a wonderful sailing tradition in the State of Wisconsin. Each yacht club sends their finest competitors. Some come from large lakes and can handle big wind. Others are tactical sailors and work well with shifting winds due to the smallness of their lakes. There are yacht clubs which have a tradition of always winning. Some have produced American Olympic Sailing Champions. People in Wisconsin and the surrounding states take competitive sailing seriously.

Sailing is a microcosm of the various economic strata found in the Midwest. Some yacht clubs are known for sailors with large, wealthy homes on premier lakes. Their parents' attire includes pressed, turned up collars and sweaters, usually not worn, but draped around the neck. I think you get the picture. Other clubs sport parents who wear tee-shirts that read: "Official Bikini Inspector". Their family may live in a small lake cottage. Some yacht club parents show up with the largest and finest SUV's made, simply to haul their brand new five-hundred pound boats to the regatta. Others have rusted pickup trucks pulling older worn, but polished boats. Despite the financial separations, these young sailors have one thing in common: they set out to win and have a burning desire to do their finest. After two months of preparation they are ready for the Super Bowl of sailing. They are true competitors; the rest of us are the court jesters. Many of them have truly enriched our lives with their friendship over the years.

As mentioned earlier, sailing provides a level field for both male and female skippers and crew. Few sports do this. In this sport, some female skippers have run circles around their male competitors. It is also a great place for young people to mingle in a safe and healthy environment. A number of these kids' parents met when they were young sailors and eventually married. Some of these ten- to sixteen-year-olds had grandparents who sailed in this event. These grandparents were part of the spectator fleet. All were excited about this end-of-the-season regatta.

The boats were polished, cleaned and ready for the first of five races. Sandy freely ran along the shore hopping and barking. She simply wanted to get on Stacy's boat and slowly worked her way into the water. Putting up the sail, Stacy was greeted by Sandy, silently bumping her boat. Deep in concentration as she prepared the ropes and pulleys, Sandy startled Stacy. "Go back, Sandy," she chided.

Sandy, just being glad to make contact, swam back to shore and shook off her water. I stood by, observing the preparation long enough to grab Sandy's wet collar. She would be a passive observer of the backyard grass for this regatta.

She knew what was coming and tried to wrestle from my grip, yelping and crying. Weighing in at close to seventy pounds, Sandy was no longer a weak puppy. She fought and twisted until I clicked the leash onto her collar. Unable to break free and now on a short leash, she shook the remaining water off her back and onto me. She barked at me in protest.

After putting her back on the leash, we got in the boat while listening to her cries and barking. They grew fainter and fainter as we started across the lake.

"Sorry Sandy, but I have another child to pay attention to," Mary Kay mumbled.

Off we went in our spectator boat. There, lining up for the start of the race, were a conglomerate of sailboats, pontoon boats, race official boats, and various gas-powered water crafts. Our kids could have been on a soccer field while we sweat on the sidelines or stood in the frozen mud. We were glad they chose sailing. We watched a beautiful scene unfold before us: cobalt blue skies with white, sun-piercing, billowing clouds. The warm winds brought the smell of boat gas across the blue green water. This smell always triggered great childhood memories for Mary Kay. For me, I preferred the smell of barbecue on the water.

Fifty-five boats jostled for position at a hundred yard starting line. Eighteen-foot masts jostled in the wind as the crisp white sails flapped waiting to be released at the starting gun. BOOM! The gun goes off and the ropes are pulled in while both young ten-or twelve-year-olds, crews and skippers, hike over the edge of the boat to help balance the wind-filled sails. Stacy takes an early lead. Life is good.

The proud parents are standing in the spectator boats, yelling for their sons and daughters as well as their yacht clubs.

"Go Cedar Lake! Go Patty!" yells a proud mom and dad. They have a reason for being involved; Patty's grandmother won the event in 1947. Others are screaming out encouragement. All are stranded on the spectator boats until the event is over. Some are not interested in the sport and are bothered by the whole event. They usually have a book and keep to themselves. Some find a good excuse for a morning cocktail.

The race is soon half over and the leaders are battling. Most parents have not taken their eyes off the race. This sport requires both strategy and luck. The boats are at the mercy of the wind, which oscillates from one side of the lake to the other. Suddenly, the wind shifts violently. We see it; will our daughter see it? Stacy does, but her competitors don't. A number of boats miss the lift of the wind.

"What is going on inside his head?" shouts an angry parent on our spectator boat. He opens another can of beer and shakes his head.

Other parents see their kids in the back of the fleet and pull out some knitting or read a paperback novel. Their kid makes sailing boring.

Not our Stacy. In a little over an hour, she holds off all challengers and noses her boat to a first place finish signaled by another gun shot. BOOM! Our spectator boat goes wild. The competition should never have allowed this to happen, but it did.

"Stacy, Stacy, wow! Way to go, Stacy!" We hug each other and high five the rest. Horns on the boats around us salute Stacy. We think they are also blowing for us, her proud parents.

Congratulating her in the finest of sportsmanship, her competitors and their parents announce, "Nice race, Stacy. Well sailed."

After all the boats finish, Stacy's win becomes short history. The boats quickly gather for the next race, but unfortunately there will be no second race: the wind has died. The boats are towed in and lunch is fed to the one hundred and ten skippers and crews. The parents spend the time catching up with old acquaintances or chiding their kids for not reading the wind properly. Having co-written the historical centennial book for the Nagawick Lake Yacht Club, my mind slips back to one hundred years earlier when the same kind of comradery was evident in the tattered photos I came across. The clothes were different, but that 'seize the day' attitude was evident in the sparkling eyes of the young competitors that day. They are all gone. Now it is our turn in the sun of the moment.

After lunch, it was back to the boats. The judges patiently waited for the wind. Nature has its own timetable. The wind was picking up slightly. It was just enough to get all the boats back out to the middle of the lake for the third race. After twenty minutes, it was evident that there would be no third race. Same reason, blue skies and no wind.

"Sailing sucks!" announces a frowning, freckled, ten-year-old crew. Rocking his boat back and forth, he has to have his boat towed back to the yacht club. Knowing that all this gear has to be packed up, then brought out again for the races the next day, who can fault his attitude? Some decide to tie their boats together and go for a swim. The boys catch the eye of some girl and a water fight begins. Two climb onto the boat of the girl of their dreams. The goal is to show her how strong they are by throwing her into the lake. This girl has been building muscles while sailing and easily tosses both boys into the water.

Heading back home, from a distance we see a yellow dot moving back and forth on our hill. The closer we get, we begin to hear the hoarse barking of an upset dog. We are greeted by Sandy barking angrily at us. She is mad. For three hours she has been left alone outside with no human contact. With her water dish long ago tipped over, we let her off her leash and she runs around the yard in circles.

Sarah shouts at Sandy, "Not all of the crazy dogs live in the nut house."

Eventually, she calms down and gets a bowl full of food from Stacy. **Food, life is good.** She never gets used to being tied up without someone around.

The second and final day of the regatta begins with a strong wind. The air is cooler and jackets are the norm. The clouds tell us rain may be on the way. Our blue skies look grey.

All of our friends are gathered, ready for the start. An eerie quiet overcomes the usually rambunctious crowd. The sailors count down the seconds until the gun goes off. They must keep their boats from going over the line before the start. The sails must be kept loose to prevent this from happening. Sails crackle in the wind. Boom! The gun goes off and the crowds on each boat start their cheering. Sails are pulled tight as the young sailors arch their backs for leverage.

Volume builds as spectators' shouts echo across the water: "Go Pewaukee Lake, Go!" "Move, Judy move!" "Get on the line, Jake!" After forty-five minutes and three trips around the buoys, Stacy has one leg left on the course and is in first place. Suddenly, the wind shifts and her nearest competitor begins to gain ground. They pass her as time seems to stretch.

"Go Stacy! Come on!" I yell. Turning to Mary Kay, I plead, "It looks like she is standing still!"

"Chuck, the wind shifted. There is nothing she can do," Mary Kay states calmly without taking her eyes off the race.

Mary Kay is our sailor. She grew up sailing on these same inland lakes. I grew up in the concrete alleys of Milwaukee with skateboards and tackle football.

Startling us, the gun sounds, horns blow, the crowd roars.

Stacy takes a third for the fourth race. It all comes down to the fifth and final race.

"Come on, Stacy! Win this one for Sandyman watching back home," shouts Sarah as she sits on the bow of the boat, knees drawn to her chest.

Like a ballet on water, the boats launch off the starting line. The sounds of the waves banging against the smooth hulls are broken by the orders and calls of the skipper to their crews, the banging of the rope toggle against the aluminum mast, and the snapping of the sails. An almost rhythmic ballet with nature providing the music. The sun is breaking through the clouds, warming the air. The blue skies return.

Battling her challengers, Stacy and her whispy nine-year old crew, Erin, position their boat to take advantage of Nagawicka Lake's shifting winds. Using a strategy of sailing off the course, Stacy gambles that there is stronger wind off the course which could propel her ahead of her competitors. There is a risk, the wind could die while you are off-course sitting with no wind, while your competition passes you by. This is called, "banging a corner". This time it works. The wind fills her sails with such momentum that when she comes back on course, she is far ahead of a number of boats. Her start was not the best. However, now she begins her move. One by one she passes the less experienced sailors. Finally, she has to beat two boats ahead of her. These are the Regatta leaders. Along the shores of the lake, the old-time sailors are listening to the call of the race on their marine radios. Stacy sailed this lake for eight years. Our 100% kid, who went to sailing school faithfully since she was five years old and practiced on her own when others were long ashore, was about to see her dream come true. This was her lake today and her time to win as she edged past the final boat fifty feet from the finish line.

BOOM! The finish gun is shot. Looking up, we see her boat with the family number and lake emblem, N-18, blazed across the sail, cross the finish line. By taking a first place, she won both the race and the regatta! Our boat erupts in an unbelievable celebration, boat horns blow across the spectator boat fleet. Proud tears well up in my eyes. Wow, I am living through my kids. I never won anything in my life except a goldfish. Now my flesh and blood has broken a twenty-eight-year dry spell for the sailors of Nagawicka Lake and, of course, her *Armenian* dad. Maybe I had one of those movie flash-backs where they show all the work the kid put in, sailing in the rain and on miserable days. That certainly was true of Stacy, but I wasn't thinking of that. This was one of those moments when you realize that it truly is a special moment and a milestone in your life. Enjoy it! We did!

Stacy and Erin come by the boat and humbly state, "We did it!"

Choking back the tears, I hug her and Erin. Mary Kay also has tears in her eyes. Wow, Wisconsin Yachting Association Champion for 2002. The grey clouds had long ago vanished; the sun was shining full now.

The boats are put away and all the sailors gather to pay homage and congratulations to the top ten finishing sailors. A beautiful, first place, engraved trophy is presented to her. The trophy contains six decades of names, each with a long forgotten story of victory.

Stacy would accept the trophy and deliver the required victory speech: "I want to say thank you to the judges, the race committee, and all the sailors who competed in this regatta. I want to thank the Lord for His strength and blessings on this day. This race is dedicated to my mom who, thirty-one years ago, took dead last in this championship"!

Mary Kay stood up and took a bow. "It's true, I did finish last," she laughed.

The crowd roared as Grandpa and Grandma looked on. This was what I would call a full circle with Grandma and Grandpa experiencing this. Grandpa was in the Navy during World War II. He was aboard the USS Sullivan, a destroyer named after the five Sullivan brothers who lost their lives as their ship was sunk by the Japanese during the early years of World War II. He fought in all the major battles of the Pacific, including Iwo Jima. His ship survived the most vicious typhoon to ever hit the United States Navy. At eighteen, he was only two years older than Stacy at that time. He reminded her that the sailing genes come from the Hajinian side of the family because of his Navy experience. Armenians are big on taking credit for great achievements and success due to genes. We knew this four hundred years before the scientists discovered genes. To be honest, it was Mary Kay's German grandparents who brought the sailing bug into the family.

We were told, by the old-timers around the lake, that they, too, had tears in their eyes as they followed the race and heard the news about Stacy's victory on their marine radios. It had been twenty-eight years of waiting, while other lake yacht clubs spoiled the party for the hosting Nagawicka Lake. The traveling trophy was now staying home. These old sailors, some in their eighties, slept well that night.

Time to get home and have the victory party. There was Sandy, her 20-foot leash wrapped around the pole with four feet left. The four-foot metal planter was knocked down spilling all the flowers for the fifth time this summer. Kari came up the steps. Sandy was out of control as she kept jumping all over Kari. Releasing her from her leash was a five-minute struggle as Sandy kept alternating licking and biting Kari's hand. She bolted down the steps to the lake to greet Stacy's boat coming into dock.

"Hey Sandyman! We won!" Stacy would scream.

Like long lost buddies, Sandy would fly off the pier landing with a big splash. Acting as a tugboat to guide the sixteen foot sailboat onto the lift, Sandy quickly scampered up the bank. Tickling Stacy's face, licks were plentiful from Sandy. Stacy laughed with zeal as she could now release all of the tension of the past two days; she had reached a pinnacle in her young life. As Sandy's tail beat quickly against the boat, Stacy hugged her wet dog. This dog, which she worked so long to get, and now she won the coveted Wisconsin Yachting Association Championship trophy – hard work paid off.

"Nice Regatta, Stacyman. You are the best," a hugging Sarah would say. All along she'd rooted for her sister with the best of them. True to Armenian form, she can be critical of her family, but if anyone else utters a word, she is ready to do battle. Stacy was her sister; if Stacy won, Sarah won. Many of the sailors and their families came to our home for a celebration party. Sandy, being the ultimate party crasher, mingled around the crowd. Wagging her tail for some, rolling on her back for others, eating fallen pieces of pizza from the grass and under the table. For those who ignored her, she simply jumped up on their chests and licked them.

"Sandy, get down!" I would yell, over and over.

"That's okay. She's a good dog, aren't you, Sandy?" proclaimed some victim while Sandy held them hostage with her outstretched paws, her wet nose and mouth.

Everyone loved this dog.

Her begging eyes conned the hardest heart as they would feed her their last morsel of cake, chips, pizza, Skittles candy and even ice cream.

Traditions are kept amongst sailors. The sailors grabbed Stacy and Erin, and threw them into the lake as part of the celebration. Sandy's ears would pin back as she slurped down some fallen ice cream before it could be recovered. She heard another invitation: splash, pause, splash, splash, the lake echoed the sounds of our girls and their friends as they jumped into the water to swim around. Within seconds, the final loud splash would be Sandy with outstretched paws, hitting the water with such force that a wake was created. The girls were blinded by the spray. Sandy could swim with the best of them. Her only problem was that she wanted to get close and give them a lick on the cheek not knowing that her paws had nails which would scratch the soft backs or arms of the fleeing girls.

They would scream, "Sandy nooo!" which would only make her more determined to get close to show her affection with a kiss.

"Ouch, no owwie. Sandy, get away," they'd cry.

Finally, the girls would get out of the water to check their scratched backs and arms, followed by Sandy.

Kari would begin wagging her finger at her. "Sandy, BAD DOG!"

Since Sandy never understood a negative word due to her selective hearing, she just shook herself until all of the water was off her hair-covered body and onto their clean dry towels. With her tongue hanging out, catching her breath, she just grinned, hiding the fact that she was or wasn't aware of her tricks. After a long day of jumping in and out, Sandy would just lay on the pier and soak up the sun in the tradition of the best Californian surfer dog from Wisconsin.

I had a great time at the party. People were dropping food like crazy. I ate so much and then drank a ton of lake water. Sure, I threw up. It was probably good for me, as I was allergic to most of that stuff. I hated to see everyone pack up their boats and cars and go. This Regatta stuff is all right, even though I was tied up. That's okay for a horse, but not me! My family was so happy with that silver cup, they didn't even notice that I pulled over the planter loaded with flowers. I sure wish I could go out on the boat with them. Other dogs can do it, so why can't I? For me, something clicks in my head. I start to breathe heavy and pace around in the car and the boat. Maybe my Labrador dad couldn't sit still either. Who knows? I am a high-energy dog. Cars and boats are not my thing. I wish they were. Lying on the grass all day gives me a rash. Bugs bother me, so I eat them. Then I get more of a rash and start scratching. The family thinks it is from people food. No way! It has to be from hanging around, lying on the grass.

Food and sex. The two things we dogs and all living things need, except me. I was spayed at six months of age. Whatever that means. I get along much better with male dogs than the female ones. Sometimes male dogs love to sniff and monkey around. I show them my teeth and they leave me alone. For me, I prefer chasing a tennis ball or running through a pile of leaves.

Anyway, Stacy had a full day and exhausted, fell asleep in bed. I know; I slept next to my 'champion'.

CHAPTER 10:

The Pier Guard

Shore Patrol

On the pier I watch fish swim around in circles. What the heck are they doing? Well, on the lake people don't swim around, they take their big pontoon boats out and drive around the lake. What kind of exercise is that? They drink lots of stuff that makes them shout and talk funny. Some shout to the Hajinians, others will wave, and some just toodle-by looking for me. Garbo says they are admiring Mary Kay's garden from a distance. I don't know about that. What's the big deal about plants? When boats came by, my job was to make myself known so they would admire me.

Sandy could care less about the intentions of those who tooled around in their boat. She was on vacation. Laying on the pier, she would not be standing guard but "laying" guard.

Everyone who came by in a boat was welcomed by a waging tail and lots of barking. If a pontoon boat got too close, within about twenty yards, Sandy was instantly in the water to greet the neighbors and their guests.

Immediately all parties were panicking: would the dog get caught in the boat propeller or would she just get run over by the boat hull? Her yellow head would stick just above the water as her shoulders pumped her sleek body through the water. Danger was this dog's middle name. She was always aware of her surroundings, somehow always able to avoid life-threatening boats and cars. It was the humans who didn't understand her quick reflexes and swift movements, so drinks would spill and people would be shouting, "Watch out for that dog! Look out!" The boat would just miss the pier. Chaos reigned. Sandy turned around and came back to the shore.

If two boats came from different directions, Sandy would swim between both. We eventually stopped yelling for her to come to the pier and simply watched the near collision she caused. Eventually, the neighbors got used to it and looked forward to Sandy's greetings.

We eventually got used to it, too. Neighbors on the lake would introduce themselves and ask about this dog that kept circling their boat. One family fell for Sandy's 'cuteness' and eventually volunteered to watch Sandy when we went away. Actually, they were strongly coerced by their young children. Given the ultimatum of either getting a dog or watching some neighbor's dog, they chose the later. Little did they know...

Constantly, the thought of Sandy being injured would weigh on us. Which reminds me of a story about the 85-year-old who was marrying the 22-year-old girl. Not to douse his enthusiasm, the family gingerly told him that at a certain age people can have a heart attack on the honeymoon. The old man, tired of being chided, simply replied, "If she dies, she dies."

So it was with Sandy. She taught us to trust her, let her go and enjoy the things of this earth. If she dies, she dies.

Sandy acted as a lifeguard anytime someone was in the water. She would bound down the seventy-five foot stairs in our backyard and sprint on the pier before leaping off into the air like a flying squirrel, surprising the unsuspecting swimmer. Usually after the initial shock, the swimmer would frantically swim away acting as if nothing had happened. Sandy simply followed the swimmer, without a noise, until she climbed on his back or was finally called back with the rewarding call: "Treat, Sandy, treat." All she wanted was to show the swimmer how well she could swim. When in Rome do as the Romans.

Tennis balls and sticks thrown into the lake would be retrieved by Sandy. Holding a four-foot stick in her mouth, she would swim back to the shore with waves and water battering her body and mouth. She loved to swim and getting ashore she would shake the water off of herself and, at times, throw up all the water that she swallowed. The pier became a mess of broken branches, wet tennis balls and at times, vomit.

Not only was Sandy a good lifeguard, she was also a helpful shore guard. Water attracts other animals, such as geese and ducks. These animals love to come ashore to rest on dry land and deposit their wastes for unsuspecting barefoot swimmers. You get the picture.

Our neighbors were constantly trying to discourage these flying fowl from fowling up their yards. Some would string up elaborate fishing line nettings so the birds could not land. Others would put plastic predator animals out on their lawn and pier. Rubber snakes, erect plastic bald eagles and owls would dot the landscapes to drive fear into these huge geese and mallard ducks. Some shorelines looked like a scene from *Wild Kingdom*, only they were poorly made plastic replicas.

We never had this problem, as Sandy chased anything that moved on the acre property. Geese, ducks, pigeons, swans, otters, muskrats and even ground hogs, were simply chased off. This was done without any barking just in case she might catch one off-guard and pounce on it. What would she do if she ever caught one? We don't know. She never caught anything except a frozen squirrel.

Asking a neighbor if those rubber owls work to drive the geese away, his response was terse, "No, they perch on the owl's head and crap all over my yard!"

Our lawn was clean, thanks to a busy yellow Lab.

CHAPTER 11:

Perfume Wonders

Treat Cookie Jar

From the dog kingdom comes the finest breed for smelling and tasting things. Through the centuries, Labradors have been bred to smell out animals for hunting and to feed their master's family or find the single piece of popcorn that fell in-between the cushions of the sofa. Sandy was no different. She would use her keen, genetic, sense of smell and eat everything, except cold-cut meats. She would eat the bread, but pass on the boloney. Makes you kind of wonder about what goes into those processed meats? Like politics, processed meats look good on the outside, but you don't want to know what goes into them. The boloney would sit at her feet. Sandy would stare at the boloney for five seconds, then look at you, look back at the meat, then back at you. She wasn't going to give that another thought. Her sense of smell was certainly different than ours.

Who wants to be full of baloney? You would just stare at them, too. I'll eat any piece of meat that was not processed. My favorite: pork chops, which I later found out, I am allergic to.

Mary Kay would tell me to put Sandy on a leash.

"It's springtime and she rolls her neck into everything, then I have to give her a bath," she'd remind me.

It's so much work to bend down, grab the leash and find the ring on her collar, I thought. "Sandy, you won't roll into anything now, will you?" I scolded her.

She wanted outside now! The cries of a yellow Lab could grab the attention of a hardened warrior. Jumping up and down like a Kentucky Derby racehorse in the stall before the race, she was too excited about going outside to hear my words even if she could! I gently opened the sliding door about a half an inch. Boom! She crammed herself through the ever-widening sliding door helping to open it like a wedge. A three-inch opening became a six-inch, then twelve and she was gone. Usually, she would spot a squirrel and chase it up a tree. Then she would look for something to put in her mouth: a shoe, an old ball, or a dried black walnut, and in the fall, oak acorns or some unidentified substance that was on the ground. She was going to a party and needed something in her mouth. This was a big problem in the winter. You could never find the matching glove or shoe until spring when the snow melted. There it was, your favorite item, sitting in the grass, soggy and ruined.

"You better get Sandy in," Mary Kay would shout over the garbage disposal. Getting up from my comfortable Lazy Boy chair, I would begin the fifteen minute ritual of getting Sandy to come home. Going outside, I would begin the shouting. "Sandy! Home!" I figured the fewer words, the less confusion. "Sandy! Home!"

Finally, she would arrive. *This time, I am in trouble.* Covered from her nose to her chest, she has wiggled in some black substance that smells so bad that the air around her almost has a different color. It must have smelled good to her, as she was smiling with her eyes and her tongue was hanging out while she panted. She couldn't have been more pleased with herself. Her tail was wagging and it looked like she way saying, "Look at me. Nice perfume, huh? I think it was 'My Mystery Smell' by some fancy European perfume manufacturer."

Fancy European perfume? You humans wear that stuff and it makes my nose itch. I think it comes from leftover boloney. I prefer the romantic smell of some black, tar-like, unnamed substance. You may call it "dead animal". How would you really know? My smell is different than yours. Who can smell a duck fifty yards away in tall grass? A human or me? I rest my case.

The good news is that she only covered herself with dirt on one side of her head. Right side: a total, tar-covered, stinking mess; left side: clean, nice, happy Sandy. I quickly led her left side past Mary Kay.

"Hi Sandy," Mary Kay says as she continues to clean.

Sandy wants to go by the sink. She pulls towards Mary Kay and lets out a emotional whine. Her tail wags faster. I pull Sandy past Mary Kay. Sandy keeps pulling toward Mary Kay to show her a new smell and body paint. Finally, I jerk her collar and whisk her up the stairs. I locate one of my daughters and in a quiet voice, tell them to get Sandy into the bathtub.

"Dad, you weren't supposed to let her loose," Kari reminds me.

A small family squabble began. "You put her out without a leash. Why do WE have to give her a bath?" Stacy questions.

Out of nowhere comes my older daughter Sarah. "Stacy, you wanted that dumb dog, so you get to give it a bath!"

Sandy just sat there, her small yellow-brown ears cocked up. Her head was tilted to one side as her lazy, almond-shaped eyes searched the faces of the fighting girls, trying to figure out what all the hub-hub was all about.

"You are not the boss, Sarah. You have to help," Stacy and Kari shout.

Obviously, there was a little tension between the girls before I arrived with Sandy.

My mother would tell me that it is good that they fight with each other, it will make them stronger for the real world. I suppose, if hand-to-hand combat comes back in vogue. My hand was beginning to change its texture due to the smell coming off of Sandy. I was getting tired of wrenching my back as I kept her from bolting.

Sarah would remind them of the 'no work or responsibility document' that she and Peter made Stacy and Kari sign before the dog came home. In the middle of these battling sisters stands Sandy, tail waging, tongue hanging out, waiting for her bath. She likes being the center of attention. The smell is now giving me visual problems.

"Ladies, get this dog in the bathtub or she goes back to the farm in Ripon!" I threatened.

Giving Sandy a bath was like trying to tame a wild bull. Soaking wet with sudsy bubbles, she would wiggle out of our grasp and try to hop the short ledge of the bathtub. After the girls would finally get her under control and rinse the shampoo out, Sandy would stand looking like a drowned rat, her eyes drooping with a false innocence. When Sandy stepped out of the bathtub, the girls were already armed and ready with a towel to throw over her sopping body before she could shake wet-dog water everywhere. Sometimes she would escape with the towel still draped on her body, running through the house like a wild animal on the loose. Rolling on the ground with laughter, the girls would try to catch her only to have her wet body and tail slip through their fingers. Shaking water all over the floor and walls, Sandy would make a mad dash back through the line of laughing girls like a bull teasing the matador. Everyone got wet. The bathroom was a mess and the tub had to be cleaned. Bath time became more challenging when the front doorbell rang and she had to see who was there without being completely dry.

I'd come running from anywhere in the house when the front doorbell rang. Imagine, some date of Sarah's, walking into our foyer. Now, facing an ever-growing yellow Labrador bolting right at him, I could smell the fear in his eyes. I had this next move down to a science. I would leap over the last few steps and land on the oriental carpet at the bottom. Using that as a spring-board, I would drive my paws into the poor boy's crotch, known as the 'danger zone', causing him to double over. This was to my advantage. Now, I could give him two quick slobbering licks on his unsuspecting face. Then I would sit on the rug, tail wagging, waiting to be in the Prom couple's pictures. Welcome to the Hajinian's home. I am Sandy!

Eventually, Mary Kay would make her way upstairs to see what all the arguing and commotion was all about. I knew my girls were no stool pigeons; they wouldn't rat on old Dad.

"Mom, Dad let Sandy outside without a leash and made US give her a bath. The bathroom is a mess, Sandy's collar still smells, and we are all wet!" they chimed in unison.

"Thanks a lot ladies, and you too, you dumb dog. Why do you have to find the worst thing out there to roll in?" I protested.

Mary Kay just shook her head, gave me one of those, 'you need to shape up' stern looks, then proceeded to rub Sandy with a towel, cooing, "Now you smell so nice, don't you?"

Sandy sat perfectly still with all of her facial expression saying, "You are the only one who understands me," Unable to contain her emotion, she gave Mary Kay a big kiss.

I took the towels downstairs and did the laundry.

CHAPTER 12:

Iron Stomach and Allergies

Banana Allergy

I have many good characteristics and behaviors that may have been overlooked. Most dogs fight when they have their teeth brushed. This involves holding my lip and cheek back with the thumb and finger. Other dogs simply nip the hands that hold them and the session is over. Toothpaste flies everywhere. And, according to my dentist, Garbo, dog's teeth need to be brushed at least twice a week. Flossing is optional. And teeth whitening for dogs is not recommended.

I sit very still and let my family brush my teeth. The reason? Peter found the chicken-flavored toothpaste. Really, it tastes great. You should try it sometime and for those of you on a diet, there are only eight calories per brushing. Trust me, after you eat all the stuff I put in my mouth, you need a thorough teeth cleaning. Try the chicken-flavored toothpaste; you can't go wrong.

Today everyone seems to have a runny nose or teary eyes. Allergy shots and medicines are a multi-billion dollar industry. People are allergic to foods, pollen and even latex rubber. Every once in a while, a patient will call me up and tell me that she thinks she is allergic to my latex dental gloves. It seems her upper lip has swollen a day after having dental work done. I thought some movie stars wanted puffy upper lips and pay thousands of dollars for such an amenity. Maybe I am doing her a favor, but she doesn't see it that way. To avoid a future lawsuit, her folder must be marked in bright red: "Latex Allergy". For her dental work I have to wear those vinyl gloves that the sandwich makers use at the local deli—great for sandwiches, but no fine motor feel, which is needed when you drill people's teeth. Allergies are everywhere.

A red mottled skin rash shows up on Sandy's leg and chest one spring. She begins to scratch until her fur is worn away. Off to the vet, Dr. Osgood, for a cure for the incessant itching. "Allergies," states the vet.

"She will itch until she breaks the skin. She should try some meds to calm the rash down," Dr. Osgood remarks. Sandy would be given the same drugs they give for heart transplant patients: prednisone, benedril, and other fun drugs.

The vet also suggested a $250 blood test to find out what Sandy was really allergic to. Vets truly care for their clients and their fees are quite reasonable when compared to human doctors. They have extensive training to go through. Whether you have a dog, a snake or some pet iguana, vets have to know the anatomy, physiology and diets of hundreds of animals and species. But, two hundred and fifty dollars?

"How about if we put Sandy in a big plastic bubble and slowly introduce things into it until she develops a rash?" I sarcastically joked.

Mary Kay rolled her eyes and told me that she'd already had it done. After a while I felt better about spending the money. Talking to myself, I said, "At least I don't have to set aside money in Sandy's college fund."

The test revealed she was allergic to grass, trees, (six different varieties), beef, turkey, pork, wheat, houseflies, mosquitoes, fish, horses, and finally cotton.

110

This created all kinds of interesting problems. One of the foremost characteristics of Labrador dogs is that they put everything in their mouths. This is the way they discover the nature of an object, because they cannot read. They have such a keen sense of smell that they are the dog of choice for the FBI. Their superior sniffing leads them to the front of water and wilderness searches for missing people.

Sandy's allergies lead us to use special lamb and rice dog food, wool towels, and no rawhide bones made of pork. Sandy rolled around in the grass all the time and trees made up about half our land. Despite our efforts, Sandy found ways of eating just about everything she was allergic to. We simply gave her medicine and called it a day.

But dogs have a great desire to eat anything. I have friends who have unbelievable stories. Their dogs have eaten Christmas ornaments, balloons, pieces of wood, stones, feminine hygiene products, leaves, socks, cell phones...you name it and some dog has eaten it. A great story accompanies all of these culinary delights. Sandy was no different. I couldn't help but think that some of these allergy problems were due to her lack of culinary discipline.

Winter brought an end to Sandy's scratching. One or two feet of snow covered every allergenic item.

At least I am not as dumb as this beagle I met at the vet. Man, did he look sad. It turned out that each morning he would go outside and eat whatever was laying around. One morning, he ate some bad, Toadstone mushrooms. Was he ever sick!

They had to hook him up to monitors and wires. What a dumb dog! Later they found out the bill! Over two thousand dollars. I believe in dog health insurance. Personally, I don't carry any health insurance, because (pause) I don't have a job.

One winter, Sandy showed up at the back door with what looked like a two-foot stick in her mouth. It turned out to be a frozen squirrel! She finally caught one of those pesky things. Thank goodness she is not allergic to dead squirrels. They would tease her relentlessly. Sandy was fast, but a squirrel can turn on a dime. Tearing through the gardens, kicking up the soil like a race horse, she would chase sometimes two squirrels at once, catching neither.

This was, as the commercial rings out, "Miller time". Sandy finally got a squirrel. Tail fiercely wagging her skinny back end while her head moved the opposite direction, Sandy proudly showed off her trophy.

"Oh no! Chuck! Come quick! Sandy has a dead animal in her mouth!" exclaims Mary Kay.

"Let's see what you've got, Sandy. Okay, let go. Release. Release Sandy!" I pleaded. She wasn't going to make it that easy. It may not have taken a lot of work catching this squirrel, but she was not giving up without a fight. A few swats on her snout didn't work. Sandy held on and blinked her eyes in anticipation of another swat.

"Close the door. You are letting all the cold air in," Mary Kay shouted.

Swats on the nose wouldn't work. Time for fast thinking. I ran to the kitchen and grabbed a handful of dog treats. Rushing outside in the freezing Wisconsin winter, I needed Sandy to make a quick decision and grab the treats in my hand. She refused to give up the squirrel. By now the wind was turning my cheeks red.

"Sandy, want all these treats?" I tempted as I threw them on the ground.

Sandy finally released the impaled treasure from her sharp teeth and grabbed the scattered dog biscuits. The frozen squirrel found a new home in the garbage can. Barking loudly in protest, Sandy followed me to the trash. She finally got a squirrel and now it had to stay in the garbage.

"Who wants to brush Sandy's teeth?" I shouted.

"Dad, we all have a lot of homework to do after we finish watching this *Lifetime* movie," chimed Sarah and Stacy.

Mary Kay called Sandy in and brushed Sandy's teeth using her favorite chicken-flavored toothpaste and our friend Jill's used toothbrushes. Jill and her husband, Bill, are great friends of Sandy. They tolerate Mary Kay and I.

Jill would pull up in her new Lexus, ring the doorbell and announce that she had more used toothbrushes for Sandy.

Rotten fruit, leaves of any kind, food from any country, rubber toys, —all were part of a 'healthy' dog diet for Sandy. During the summer months there exists a period that lasts a week when the june bugs come out. They are flying and sometimes crawling, orange-red bugs, about the size of a pecan. They give off a pungent odor and fly around making a nuisance of themselves. This happens at night; I think it has something to do with their mating habits. Anyway, one kept flying around the house and made the girls scream. Sandy comes running into the kitchen and notices the bug buzzing and crawling on the floor. *A new toy*, she thought. Her paws began playing with it. The bug tries to get away and Sandy follows it. This is getting fun! The bug is losing the battle. After Sandy tired it out, she simply ate it. Apparently, she was not allergic to june bugs. Flies, yes; june bugs, no.

"Gross! Sandy ate the bug," screamed Kari.

When we first moved into our home, which is half woods and half lawn, Kari would do an Indian war dance in fear each time she

113

saw a bug. We were used to the screams. As bad parents, we would ignore her cries. After all, what harm can an ant cause on the concrete patio? Not so with Sandy.

Bugs became Sandy's specialty. She could eat a moth right out of the air. Ants were consumed. Even flies avoided her. Eventually, eating bugs would lead her to vomit. The substance looked like it was from another planet. This mess was left on the grass, bed, carpet, and any place her stomach told her to. Long ago, when I said *okay* to getting Sandy, I knew this would happen. I simply learned to live with stains on the carpet and bedcovers. My American-Armenian relatives just shook their heads in disbelief. "He is 'Ghent teh', translated, "a little mentally off balance."

"Ack. Ack. AACCK!" Out it would come and then, the ever-wagging tail. Sandy was off for more delightful culinary treats.

More difficult to control were the visits and feedings she got at all the neighbors' houses. Sandy would visit each house. Sitting nicely in the neighbor's house four doors away, Sandy would wait patiently for Heidi (who didn't know of Sandy's pork allergies) to give her a piece of her pork sandwich. After a moment, her patience would begin to wear thin. The contained energy would build up until she could no longer hold it in. (Perhaps if we could harness that energy, we could light up our house.) Her front paws would do a little shuffle and her tail would dance a little. Sandy's soft green eyes would follow you as she sat there at attention. Like a food soldier, she sat at attention, with no expression until you said, "Okay." Then she would gently, but quickly, grab the food out of your hand and with two chews she was done. With the precision of the finest neurosurgeon, she could remove the tiniest food sample wedged between your fingers without drawing blood. A quick swallow and she would be sitting, waiting for the next morsel to drop. I called it aerobic eating: swallowing without chewing.

Each neighbors' house had a different food story. Soon enough, the kids of the neighborhood would come running, laughing as they told us that Sandy, while in their house, had eaten socks. Cotton socks, the allergy special, ack, ack, scratch, scratch, all over again. Her legs would get scratched and bitten until the hair was gone and her pink skin showed through.

Sandy liked to quietly sneak up the stairs and explore the bedrooms. This exploration was not to find the source of the Mississippi like Lewis and Clark. No, this was a hunt for something to digest. What was she eating now? Standing at the foot of the steps and calling her name was futile. A ring of the cookie jar usually brought her bolting down the steps with the offending object, half chewed, sticking out of her mouth.

"Release Sandy!" would be the command.

She was smart. The hostage underwear was not leaving her mouth until she saw the dog treat, OUT OF THE COOKIE JAR.

All I get to eat is dog food. I wonder what goes into that dog food. I have to eat these pellets, which are dry and crunchy. The same thing every day. My stomach craves variety. I am an intelligent dog who needs to supplement her diet. Roughage is good for your body. The food bag, I am told, reads, "Proper balance between fat and protein, highly digestible for small, compact stools for easy cleanup." I finally figured out why they feed me that stuff. How selfish! The cleanup crew gets compact stools.

CHAPTER 13:

Sandy's Friendly Vet: Dr. Osgood

Dr Osgood, Maggie and Opal

Recently, there was an interesting story in *Reader's Digest* about a ventriloquist and a blond woman. It seems that the ventriloquist was wrapping up his comedy routine with a blond joke. Before he could finish, a blond woman stands up in the middle of the crowd and shouts, "I am tired of people insulting the intelligence of blond women. Just because someone has light-colored hair does not make them any less than a human being!"

The ventriloquist was frozen. He began to stumble out an apology. "I didn't ah, mean to, um, offend you..."

Before he could finish, the blond woman, pointing her finger at the wooden dummy, shouts, "I'm not talking to you, I'm talking to that guy on your lap!"

Dr. Darlene Osgood is a blond, but far from the one in the joke. She is a beautiful and intelligent woman who happened to be Sandy's dedicated veterinarian. Her enthusiasm for animals is extraordinary. So are her stories. Each time we would call her with a question about Sandy eating this or that, she had a reassuring answer and a *one better* story. One of her stories involved a ninety-pound Doberman pincher, named Dino. It seemed that Dino ate just about anything. One day Dino stopped eating and began to vomit. The family had been through this before and knew what to do, and so did

Dr. Osgood. Everyone knew what to do simply because this was Dino's third surgery in four years. Dino was prepared for abdominal surgery to retrieve some object that wouldn't pass. The only excitement was discovering what Dino had eaten now. It wasn't the usual dress sock or underwear. This time he'd swallowed a pair of pantyhose that stretched out, were four feet long. He was back on his feet in a day or two and romping around within a week.

'George the third', a Cocker mix, had a urinary tract infection. X-rays revealed stones in the bladder. Dr. Osgood explained, "In reviewing the X-rays, I noticed something in the stomach. It was definitely a foreign object. During the surgery to remove the bladder stones, I opened the stomach and to my amazement found a tube of chapstick, one maiden form bra label and thirty-six cents in change!"

The family was not surprised. George had a habit of eating coins anywhere he could find them. When company would leave, he would sniff the cushions for loose change or sniff the floor in the car. Dr. Osgood offered to deduct the thirty-six cents off of her $1800 bill.

The family responded, "Keep it as a down payment on the next surgery."

We would complain to Dr. Osgood about Sandy's habit of chewing and ruining our good shoes. Costs were mounting. Dr. Osgood, always with a one better story, relates how a Burmese Mountain dog, "Pepper", claimed an expensive couch as her domain. These dogs are very large and some of the most expensive dogs in the world. Pepper stretched out on the couch making it her hangout. One day her owner sat on the couch next to her while he worked on his brand new laptop computer. Pepper, being territorial, put up with it until her master left to answer the phone. When the owner came back, good old Pepper had shredded the soft computer screen with her claws. Lesson learned: never place anything on Pepper's couch.

"Sandy is a great dog, at least she doesn't steal food off the table," Doctor Osgood continued. Ralph, a year-old sheep dog, and Bailey, an eight-year-old Wheaten terrier, were two partners in crime. It seems six uncooked bratwurst were stolen off the grill. The owners called me and asked what to do." She continued, "I told them uncooked meat was not the best thing for a dog. They needed to induce vomiting by giving the dogs hydrogen peroxide. The only question was which dog swallowed the bratwurst?"

Since neither confessed and both looked guilty, hydrogen peroxide was administered to both dogs.

Poor Ralph had to throw up along with Bailey. After a few 'ack, acks,' Bailey turned out to be the guilty one."

Dr. Osgood had a list of things dogs had eaten. Some have passed, some needed surgery to retrieve: underwear, pantyhose, socks, jewelry, including necklaces, earrings, gold chains, diamond wedding rings, silverware, plates, ceramic fish, rare coins and other non-organic items. One wealthy grandmother was up from Florida visiting her family and their new chocolate Labrador puppy. When she leaned over to pet the cute little dog, her diamond pendant and gold cross slid down her neckchain and dangled before the puppy's ever-widening eyes. Within seconds they were part of his digestive system. Due to the outrageous cost of these items, the family followed "Chips" around with a bag and shovel for two days.

Probably the best story involves a two hundred and twenty-five pound St. Bernard named "Bruiser". Bruiser liked to dig in the yard, which most dogs like to do. Dig a hole in the yard, bury a bone. Bruiser didn't bury anything. He dug up the biggest rock he could find and proceeded to swallow it. This happened four times. Each time requiring a three thousand dollar surgery to remove the boulders. Non-dog owners would be shaking their heads at stories like these. They only show how much dogs become part of the family and how far people will go to preserve the love they have for these four-legged animals.

Dr. Osgood's story continues, "Dogs will eat any kind of food with no limit. My yellow Lab, Maggie, ate one and a half pounds of bread in one sitting. There she lay, stomach bloated. Occasionally, Maggie would whine with discomfort and glance at her swollen belly with a perplexed look: *Where did this thing come from, how did this happen?*'

One of Dr. Osgood's most expensive cases involved a beloved German Shepherd who had eaten so much food and drunk so much water, his stomach twisted. This put pressure on his spleen, which in turn caused cardiac problems. When all was said and done, the bill for the dog specialists, hospital stay and the surgeries was $17,000. "Ralph" did fine; his master had to cancel his family's European vacation.

A local business executive told Dr. Osgood his story of the world's most expensive dog. One morning his children's babysitter knocked on the door with a small dog in her arms. It seems the dog had been hit by a car and the babysitter did not have the $75 to take it to the vet. The executive's children pushed open the door and immediately fell in love with the cute dog. They took the dog out of the babysitter's hands and brought it in to play. Tom thought the dog looked fine and could walk. He knew his kids wouldn't let go of it. He told the babysitter that his family would look after the stray she found. After about an hour, the dog began to have convulsions. The children cried, something had to be done. They found a vet in the area and brought the dog in. After a series of X-rays, it was determined that the dog had a ruptured spleen and would need surgery. The X-rays, exam and blood work were about $400. The surgery to repair the partially torn organ was difficult. The dog would have to remain overnight at the animal hospital. The surgery and overnight care would be close to $1,800. By morning, Tom was called to the hospital. The dog had died.

The vet asked how he would like the dog's remains cared for. He began to recite the options: "For $800 we can perform an autopsy and have the dog buried in a local pet cemetery, for $550 we can provide cremation services with an urn for his ashes." The executive, reeling from the cost, tells the vet that he will bury the dog in his backyard.

"This would be allowed in most counties, except Pewaukee, Wisconsin, where it is against the law to bury a dog on private property," explained the vet.

"Okay, I will pay for cremation services," Tom says with his hand on his forehead.

Wincing his face, the vet responds, "Sorry, our crematorium is out of service this week."

The total bill was $3,000 for the twenty-three-hour dog. At least the family got to visit the gravesite at the pet cemetery.

With stories like those, I was beginning to appreciate Sandy's good nature. She never stole food from the table to the best of our knowledge. "Missey", the yellow Lab, another patient of Dr. Osgood's, used to open the donut box, take out a Krispy Kreme, close the lid and hide. Missey's owners always knew that something illegal was eaten when they found Missey under the dining room table.

Not all of the things that dogs eat cause expensive problems. Our neighbors, Mary and Jeff, have a Lassapoo named 'Napoleon'. It seems that Napoleon has a paper fetish. He loves to unravel and eat toilet paper. Dr. Osgood told them to hide the toilet paper, but not to worry. Napoleon then sought out paperback books. The covers, especially the romantic ones, were eaten or shredded.

Another friendly veterinarian, David, told me stories about his Poodle named 'Charlie'. Charlie chewed the cork out and consumed a half bottle of Grand Mariner. Everyone got a kick out of the inebriated dog as he swayed and lurched around the room. Later they discovered the rest of the bottle contents made a sticky mess in the carpet.

David continued, "We have an X-ray of a dog's belly where the owner had witnessed him eat a bottle cap. Not just one, but three were seen on the X-ray. After surgery, I returned the caps to their rightful owner. He recognized them as from the last three months of sample beers from his 'Beer of the Month' club. One had been in the stomach for at least two months and was still fresh enough to read the label."

One afternoon, the then three-year-old Sandy gave her master a scare. Mary Kay found a torn apart battery packaging. One double-A battery was missing. "Sandy, come here!" Mary Kay demanded. Sandy, head down, slowly entered the kitchen with her tail lowly whispering back and forth. "What happened to the battery? Did you eat this?" snapped Mary Kay. Sandy now sat down and licked Mary Kay's hand. She wasn't talking. Calling Dr. Osgood, Mary Kay got an earful of the possible complications of a dog swallowing a battery. Chemical leakage and bowel obstruction being the two major ones. Sandy was rushed into Dr. Osgood's office. She immediately ran to the scale and sat on it.

"Come on Sandy, up on the table," Dr. Osgood cooed.

Nothing doing without a treat. Finally, after a dog treat, Sandy left the scale and leaped onto the table. After a series of X-rays: head, neck, chest, and abdomen, the battery was not to be found. The verdict was in, not guilty, cleared by X-ray evidence. Sandy panted and scratched hard at her left ear. All was not lost, she had a left ear infection which was treated at the same time.

CHAPTER 14:

Fall Mischief With Eleanor

Partners in Crime

Sometimes in life you find a friend who doesn't have much in common with you. She may be of the opposite sex, or comes from the wrong side of the road. She may be a different size and wear a much smaller collar than you. Perhaps she may be even be a different breed. If the dog was human, he or she would be your golfing buddy or your poker friend. Like the great comediennes, Abbott and Costello, something clicks. You play off of each other.

Hey Garbo, I've got a friend like that. You know, your dog buddy knows what you are thinking before you bark. Sharing the same eating interests, you hunt for the same smelling stuff in the neighborhood. With different smelling abilities, you compliment each other as you find dead animals and rotten leaves for "rolling in it purposes". That was my Border Collie neighbor, Ellie.

A dog either loves or hates other dogs.

It can tell at first glance whether it has met a new playmate or an arch enemy. It can greet a fellow dog with the hair on its back standing straight up, followed by a deep growl and bark, or sniff body parts with its tail waging. Sandy had her share of both encounters: the growling and the sniffing. One of Sandy's favorite dogs lived across the street and was named Eleanor. Ellie for short.

Ellie was a miniature Border Collie that was half the size of Sandy. Any mention of Ellie's name would make Sandy go crazy. She would run around in circles, barking and whining. If that didn't work, she would jump up and down, and continue her whining. If she spotted Ellie going for a walk through the dining room window, look out. Barking, whining, twirling, jumping all at the same time. Opening the door, Mary Kay would expel, " Okay, go outside!" With the enthusiasm of baseball fans rushing the field after a World Series win, Sandy would bound out the door and within seconds stand in front of Ellie, nose-to-nose with their tails wagging in rapid unison. True friendship!

These two became partners in crime. Raiding the squirrel feeders set out by another neighbor became a fine vacation spot. They would come home with corn on the cob, minus the corn. Birdseed and other delights were there for Ellie and Sandy to raid. Some neighbors did not find this cute. One particular neighbor, who lived next door to Ellie, was not too excited about these bandits. Scolding would come. After the lecture, these two would simply begin wagging their tails and come home.

One Christmas I bought a ten pound bag of birdseed and took it over as a peace offering to that particular neighbor. The card read, "Merry Christmas. Sorry, we can't help ourselves," signed Sandy and Ellie. Eventually, they stopped going over there. All was well, the sun continued to rise in the east, and this neighbor came to tolerate and even pet these dogs. We began to find out more about her and her family. Her grandchildren would come to visit. The highlight of such a visit was to pet Sandy, the dog across the street.

"E - llie, Eleanor, E-L-I," Sarah would tease Sandy.

She wouldn't say the name Eli, simply because it would cause the circus act to begin. This was an intelligence test for Sandy. How close could you get to saying her name without actually saying it.

"Elo, Elm tree, Eleanor," Sandy would cock her head. One short ear would raise up. This went on for ten minutes.

Finally, Peter would shout, "Sarah, stop teasing the dog!"

From the age of three, Sarah had Peter's number. She knew how to rile her older brother to no end. When Peter was six, he played army man like most boys his age. The only problem was three year old Sarah had his toy gun.

"Give me the gun Sarah," he would kindly plead.

Unable to say the word gun, her retort was immediate and forceful: "My gum."

She meant it. Teasing time began. Peter would let out an exacerbated sigh. Sarah and he both knew he wasn't getting the "gum". Now Sarah had two to tease: one, an animal; the other, her brother. Going to the cookie jar, which contained the coveted treats, she would rattle the lid. Sandy would bound down the stairs from some bedroom, or up from the basement, to stand one foot from the counter, tail wagging, intense eyes watching for the hand to enter the cookie jar to bring out a treat.

This time Sarah was the master. "What Sandy? What do you want? I don't have anything."

Labs are patient animals. They can sit in a hunting blind waiting for the right time to flush out the ducks for as long as it takes. Quietly, not moving a muscle, they could wait. No deep breathing, panting, tail wagging. They are frozen in the moment of time while they concentrate on the reward ahead. So it was with Sandy.

If Sarah is going to just stand by the cookie jar and mumble some mumbo jumbo, I can wait her out, thought Sandy.

Squatting down, Sandy would sit and stare at Sarah, waiting for some weakness. Staring right at her, eye-to-eye contact. *If you don't give me a treat, you will feel miserable. Look into my green eyes. You are getting sleepy, sleepy...give the dog the treat...give the dog the treat...* Sandy's look could project across the room.

Finally, policeman Peter would break the stalemate, "Mom, Sarah's teasing Sandy again."

Sarah would laugh. Mary Kay would scold her and give Sandy a handfull of treats for being so good and not simply biting Sarah.

One late winter afternoon at dusk, our neighbor across the street rang the doorbell. Mary Kay found a concerned look on her face as she let her in.

"Ellie is missing," she said, choked with emotion.

"What do you mean?" Mary Kay asked.

"We haven't been able to find her for the last hour. We have scoured the usual spots. This is not like her to disappear," Karen told us with a very concerned look on her face.

"Is Sandy around?" she asked.

Mary Kay looked around and asked Stacy, "Where is Sandy? She was just sitting by the front door chewing on her rubber ball?"

Gone. Not to be found. This dumb dog didn't even leave a note, like, "Going to hang out with Eli, probably be a few miles away, don't worry, took the charge card." They would wander a few hundred feet away, raid the squirrel feeder next door, explore some garbage cans in someone's garage—that's about all. This time they were off the block no where to be found.

Shouting, "Sandy, Ellie," Mary Kay and Karen hunted for their lost children.

Perhaps they ventured out on the frozen lake. There were soft spots on the ice where they could have gone down. The lake in the winter can be treacherous for the unsuspecting soul. Many times, Sandy would venture out on the frozen wasteland chasing a blowing leaf or going to bother the ice fishermen. There were soft pockets in the ice that would simply break through. Fearing the worst, we ventured along the shoreline calling their names and looking for the flash of movement as the winter sun set and the shadows were beginning to fall. Karen, cheeks red with tears, kept blaming herself for not keeping her on a leash. This was (Faustian bargain) a Catch -22 problem. You want them to have their freedom, but you don't want to pay the emotional consequences for the problematic events that may occur. Mary Kay would encourage her, "These are smart dogs. They are probably just chasing squirrels nearby."

A frantic phone call to the Delafield Police brought only a sighting by one of the officers of two dogs walking in downtown Delafield—four miles from home. There was little we could do. About an hour later, a familiar sight appeared in the driveway. There was Sandy, tail between her legs, slowly walking up the driveway. She knew she was in trouble.

"Where were you?! Bad dog!" chimed Kari and Stacy.

Sarah stood at the treat jar and rattled the top. Sandy's head perked up and she ran into the kitchen.

"Ohhhh! No treat for you! Bad dog!" Sarah scolded. "You think we have treats for dogs who run away with strange dogs and don't bother thinking about us? Well, guess again buster. You eat your dry dog pellets!" She couldn't resist the opportunity to educate this wandering dog.

An hour later, Ellie showed up to the cheers and scolding of Karen and her family. From that day on, we became close with Karen and her husband. When you take the time to get to know your neighbors, you discover how connected everyone really is. As Sandy and Ellie would run around together, I began a conversation with Ellie's owner, David. I discovered that Dave's father was the famous wrestler from the 1950's through the 1970's known as the "Crusher". In fact, my father went to school with him at South Milwaukee High School in the 1940's. My uncle even had a crush on his mom at the same high school. Luckily, my uncle was so painfully shy that he could never approach her. Otherwise, Dave might be my cousin and be forced to attend Armenian family functions.

It didn't really matter. Sandy and Ellie just had a ball exploring, and with our watchful eye, keeping them from leaving the neighborhood.

CHAPTER 15:

Sleepovers
for the 'Orphan'

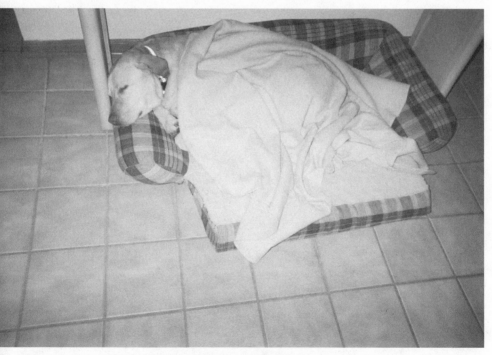

Dog Treat Dreams

"These dentures you made for my wife make her look like a monkey!" complained an irate husband.

With your apelike features, it is a perfect match, I thought, but dared not say. "She seems to like them, but I will do what I can to change them," I simply replied.

Time for a vacation after a day like that. Dentistry has lots of advantages, dealing with an angry public is not one of them. There are times I wish I could snap back. For example, when the mean, high strung 'account executive type' asks what can be done about her yellow teeth, I want to say, in my best Rodney Dangerfield impression, "Wear a brown dress!" But I cannot. Too many people have had too many bad experiences going to the dentist. Due to all this bad history, dentists have to be ambassadors of good will EACH AND EVERY DAY! All the stories I hear from people make me think that either they are using these "bad experiences" as an excuse to not care for their teeth, or these dentists actually attended a 'Hitler Youth Camp' for their training. Either way, I needed a break.

A quick phone call to Mary Kay and we were ready to head away for a few days when the kids were off from school. One problem was Sandy. She absolutely hated traveling in a car. We loathed being in the car with her. She would move from the back seat to the front, then over to the corner window. Squeaking and crying, while drool flew from her mouth, was not my idea of a fun ride. She also liked to force her body between myself and the steering wheel, which is okay, except when you are traveling at seventy miles an hour on the expressway. This was a seventy-pound dog who must have had a problem with motion that she, herself, was not creating.

What were we to do with her? Mary Kay made a few calls and found two families just begging to watch her for a few days. When we brought out our suitcases, she would start to whine and look real sad, head down, slowly moving her eyeballs from one side to the next. How dare we go!

She would soon forget about us. Staying at our neighbor's house, two doors down, Sandy played with their two daughters and young son. Sandy knew we were going away and to retaliate; she simply ate their socks. Not one or two, but seven in a day! The girls were constantly chasing Sandy around to get their socks out of her mouth. *Finally, some attention*, she must have thought. We never asked what happened to those socks.

In the evening she would sleep at the foot of the bed of their parents' room. Kids are great for dogs, but it is the adults who replenish the water dish and fill the food bowl. Ricky, the young son, would carry treats around in his pocket to keep Sandy's undivided attention. He had her number. She would gently follow him around while he jingled those treats in his pocket, occasionally giving her one to swallow.

Another family was being bugged by their two young children for a dog. So, they simply asked to watch Sandy for a weekend and help the kids 'get it out of their system'. Big mistake.

We packed up Sandy's belongings. She sensed that we were leaving and she was going somewhere. She wasn't her usual self, all excited about going out the front door. She simply waited to see what happened.

We loaded up the van and finally called Sandy. "Come on, Sandy. We are going bye-bye." Jumping into the van, she immediately used her superior smelling abilities to find a McDonald's French fry wedged below the back seat cushion. Three miles later, we pulled up to the house. Sandy was greeted by Margery and Robbie, a nine- and eleven-year-old. They hugged Sandy and helped bring her things into the house. With her tail wagging, she followed her only possessions: her bed, blanket and assorted chew toys.

As we left, she saw what was coming, bolted out the door and sat by the car. She liked the kids, but did not want to be dumped again. Her favorite place to sleep was Kari's bed, since Stacy spent the whole night hugging and squeezing her. Sandy must have been concerned about what these kids would do when she fell asleep? A few treats later, Sandy was inside the house, playing with a tennis ball, to the hugs and pets of her newfound friends. We were on to our well deserved vacation.

The two kids, Margery and Robbie, had a blast. It seemed that Sandy wanted to play all day and night. Robbie had a group of guy friends for a sleepover. He asked if they could sleep on the couch next to Sandy. With his parents okay, Robbie fell asleep while Sandy played. Waking up in the morning, all of the boys found their faces wet with slobber. Sandy gave each one a good-night, facial lick.

Arriving to pick up the distracted dog, Sandy dropped everything and came running. There she sat at the car, not being tricked by the doggy treat anymore. We thanked them for the care they gave to our dog. They looked up at their mom and dad with the Academy Award sad eyes and said nothing. We could feel the parents' guilt as we drove away.

That was a sleepover! I just love kids cause they are just like me. They have no fear about feeding me just about anything. They also are low to the ground and give great hugs. I need love. I am not ashamed to admit that a hug feels good. I also like belly scratches. Sometimes I rub my back on some rough carpet AND get a belly rub at the same time. Those kids had more energy than me. When the treats ran out, I just lay down and rested. After they all fell asleep, I found myself eating all kinds of stuff hidden in their couches. Pretzels, marshmallows, some sticky candy, hard French fries and the "mystery object". Garbo thinks I am nuts. At least I am more in control than my Lab friends, Dune and Cazador.

One weekend, Dave and Eddi went an hour away for dinner leaving their dogs for four hours. Upon returning, Dune looked bloated. Acting guilty with a sad look on his face and moving low to the ground, they discovered why. He had taken the top off the 15 gallon, food storage bin and eaten the full bag of dog food until he was bloated. Taking him for a walk until he had three bowel movements, they made Dune sleep in the garage. Cazador, their chocolate Lab, did not indulge in the binge eating. However, he was also punished by being made to sleep in the garage. Cazador got revenge by eating a tennis ball during the night. The next day, Cazador would not eat breakfast or dinner. The following day he still wouldn't eat. For a Lab, this means something is really wrong. There is no such thing as an anorectic Labrador dog.

The vet said he must have eaten poison fertilizer. After more tests, they thought he had pancreatitis. Then he was taken to another hospital for more tests and X-rays. Finally, the vet came back with the diagnosis for my surgeon friend's dog: he has a bowel obstruction and needs surgery amounting to $1,500 to be paid up front. Dave, as a surgeon, thought that perhaps he could get a new dog for half that amount.

His wife, however, had another idea. "I don't want to tell the boys that we didn't do everything to save that dog."

Dave, in the meantime, was called in to remove a bowel obstruction for an eighty-one-year-old lady. The removal was successful and the lady did just fine.

Eddi gave the nurse her charge card. In the middle of the surgery, the doctors found a tennis ball that had been unraveled and caught up in Cazador's stomach. The surgeon would come out of surgery and explain that they would need another $500 down to finish the surgery. Eddi paid. Dave was paid $400 from Medicare and had to wait three months to be paid for saving the lady's life. Cazador's recovery went well. After a few weeks, he was up to his usual game of chase the object into the lake. Dune forgot about his food binge.

Dave kept whining about the reimbursement discrepancy between his work on humans and the vet's charges. Eddi, laughing, gave Dave the latest plumbing bill for a clogged toilet. "Here Dave, quit whining and look at this one."

The bill read: "Unplug one toilet, plus trip charge: three hundred twenty-five dollars."

"Dave, this guy said he was a drain surgeon," Eddi smiled.

Dave winced and put his hand to his forehead. Just then, Cazador pushed a tennis ball into his crotch. He wanted to play 'get the tennis ball' with Dune.

 CHAPTER 16:

The Neighborhood Stripper

Hi

One afternoon while raking leaves and talking with my neighbor Jim, who lives two doors away, we were interrupted by my next-door neighbor, Gunar. It seems he was having a bachelor party for one of his friends and gave us each an invitation with the hint of a semi-nude stripper on the front of the invitation. The party was tonight at seven and the entertainment was "Wanda" the exotic dancer. We thanked him and chuckled: like we would be allowed to go to a party like that. You see, our wives controlled our social calendar; and chips, dip and strippers were not their idea of healthy entertainment. You see, I have high cholesterol, and chips and dips are not on the diet.

The naked human body is a wonderful thing. I have taken sketch and painting classes where there was a live naked model for the anatomical study of muscle, skin tones and posture. It is hard to lust after the model when you are mixing paints and trying to see negative space shadows. Besides, when everyone is done, you want to present a beautiful painting or drawing, showing your ability to observe subtle light and tone changes in the skin, not some scratchy lines with drool on the paper.

Coming into the house, I placed the invitation on the counter and within six minutes was summoned by my wife to explain what this was all about.

"Well, Gunar is having a bachelor party for a friend and he invited Jim and me. There will be lots of food and stuff," I explained with a chuckle.

Mary Kay's response was quick and sharp: "You are not going to that party!" I didn't need her words, her facial expression said it all.

The time of the party was about 7:30 p.m. At 7:15 p.m., a squirrel ran across the large patio door and sent Sandy into a tizzy. She yelped with the need to chase that animal. *What's with these animals needing to chase each other all the time, I thought. We don't chase them.* Even joggers stay on a path and don't chase after a deer or other joggers.

"Sandy, sit!" I yelled. After three minutes of jumping, barking and whining, I finally decided to let Sandy out so I could enjoy the ballgame. I opened the door three small centimeters, just enough to get a finger through and grab the chain to put on Sandy's neck. She would have nothing to do with a chain; she wanted that squirrel! Moving me out of the way and pushing her nose through the opening, she forced open the sliding patio door and was gone.

"Sandy!" I shouted.

She followed the squirrel, you guessed it, right next door. She never made it quite next door. The squirrel ran up a tree. With me running after her, Sandy spotted a woman coming up the driveway with high-heel pumps and a raincoat on, and that's about all. Sandy found the "entertainment" for the bachelor party and was jumping up on her raincoat as it flew open. I was twenty feet behind and kept yelling, "Sandy, get down! Sorry about the dog." By now the stripper was petting Sandy on the head and bending over to rub Sandy on the belly. She just laid on the pavement with her paws folded up, tail brushing against the asphalt.

144

I quickly put the leash on Sandy and tried not to look at the merchandise. Apologizing profusely, I turned around to take Sandy home and spotted Mary Kay in the yard, observing the whole thing. The stripper smiled and with her hands on her hips, watched me drag Sandy home. "Bye Sandy," the woman cooed. Sandy tugged on the leash towards her as if she was being separated from some long lost relative. She squeaked and barked in rebellion. Her paws dug into the grass as I struggled to get her home.

"You planned that, didn't you?" Mary Kay smirked. "You had to let Sandy out right at seven fifteen, didn't you? And why didn't you put her on the leash?"

I just chuckled and smirked at Sandy. "I guess this means we can't go to the bachelor party and have chips and dip, Sandy. Thanks a lot, you dumb dog!"

Sandy just looked at the tree and then the driveway, and panted, probably thinking, "Life is good. A new person petted me."

Garbo, my thoughts exactly! Dogs don't drool over naked people. I am always naked! Dogs see their buddies' naked butts all the time! You know, when you can get over the 'naked' part, the dancer needed me to come over and be her friend. Her eyes seemed to be a little sad and tired. Was that a tear in her eye and a 'sigh' on her lips? It didn't matter, Sandy is here.

When she rubbed my belly, she got a twinkle in her eyes and a big smile on her face. Who can resist a pretty and soft yellow Lab like me?

CHAPTER 17:

Sarah's Kidney Stones

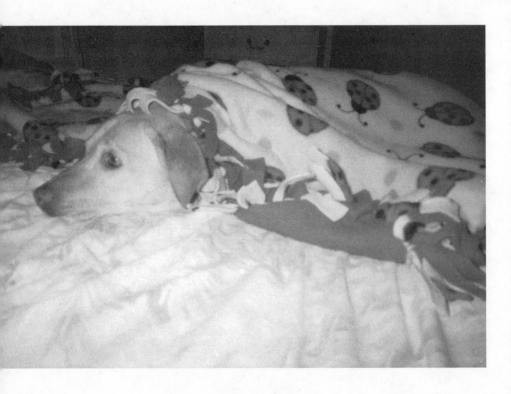

Just Take it Easy

My aunt always says, "What goes around, comes around." She would always tell me it in Armenian and remind me that this is what my grandmother taught her. You would have to accept advice from a Harvard professor and my immigrant grandmother. Since I don't know any Harvard professors and my grandmother is no longer with us, my aunt takes the role as the advice giver. The problem is, "What goes around, comes around" is really a summary of the literal Armenian saying, "If you do a good deed, a fish will return to the water." Obviously, it doesn't work in English. That is why we have my aunt. I think she means that when you sign a contract for not caring for a dog, sometimes it comes back to haunt you. For example, Sarah, the one who signed a contract against helping with Sandy, learned how truly comforting Sandy could be.

One evening the family had scattered to their various entertainment venues: Mom and Dad to dinner with friends, Stacy at her basketball game, and Kari was sleeping at a friend's house. Peter was away at the University of Wisconsin for his sophomore year of college. The house was kept alive by Sarah and Sandy.

For two days, Sarah had a sore throat and had consumed very little of anything, including water. She was in her bed and experienced the sharp pain, her first of many, kidney stone attacks.

So, I almost had the house to myself, and I was enjoying the quiet house that I now had control over. I think I was scratching behind my left ear when I heard crying upstairs. Let me back up. I was in the dining room looking out the window for somebody or an animal to bark at. I am usually fed at this time, but since no one was home, my bowl sat empty. Because my vet, Dr. Osgood, said I was getting fat, my family limited my feeding to once a day. I must protest! First of all, I am not that fat. Dogs get bigger as they get older. And so what if I am getting a little rounder? I don't wear clothes or have to squeeze through some opening like a cat. I believe there is something in the Geneva convention about feeding a dog more than once a day. If I could read, I would look it up.

Back to Sarah. She was my only hope to get a full bowl of food. I bounded up the stairs. My keen ears heard her moaning and cries from her room. I slowly walked into the room and put my paws up on her bed about two inches from her face. Then I put my wet nose next to hers and let out a sigh, just so she would know that I was there. I sensed that she had a stomach ache. Where were her parents? How could they leave this sick girl all alone? This was getting to be the worst night of my life!

Sarah said that Sandy's expressive eyes showed concern and her arching eyebrows showed Sandy's confusion over what was happening.

I was confused about all of this crying. I mean, she thought she had problems! I was the one starving, except for some snacks I found under the couch. Hunger can block our emotions. I was about to go get my bowl to get her attention, but Sarah was in such pain she was drawing her knees up to her chest. Before I could present my case to her, she grabbed my head and pulled my whole body onto the bed next to her. As she sobbed, she held onto me and her spasms seemed to stop. I began to see that she really needed me more than I needed to be fed. I licked her face six

times. I think it made her forget about her pain. I lay there real still as she hugged me real hard.

Mary Kay and I came home. There was no yellow Lab to jump up on us. Something seemed wrong. We knew Sarah was home.

"Mom, Dad, I am up here!" Sarah shouted.

Bounding up the stairs, we found our teary-eyed Sarah.

"I have a bad kidney stone," she cried.

Straining to be released was Sandy, held tightly by Sarah. Mary Kay put her arm around Sarah and felt her forehead for a fever. Sandy let out a bark.

Mary Kay gave Sandy a big hug. "Good dog, Sandy. Are you protecting Sarah? Good DOG!"

You bet I am a good dog, and where were you guys? Don't let this wagging tail fool you. Can't you hear my barks? I am more than upset. Where were you? Here we are with an emergency and I don't know how to use a phone. At least you guys finally got her some help. She got some medicine and water. Whatever they did worked, and she got back to normal. I get pills, too. For my efforts, I got a good meal of dog pellets and a few treats for which I had to perform lots of tricks like sitting still and raising a leg (I think you call it giving a paw).

Afterwards, we sat as a family and watched television. Sandy rested her head on Sarah's lap as she scratched Sandy's ears. From that day on Sarah had a special bond with Sandy and volunteered to help with her chores. As we sat on the couch, Sarah's kidney stone passed and the color returned to her face. Sandy was unusually quiet as we watched television as a family. Sandy seemed distant, perhaps the moving images of television were hard for her to follow.

151

No television for me. I usually stand in the dining room, looking out the window at the gardens and the road. Waiting, just waiting for another dog walking a human to come by. Sometimes I see my favorite human neighbor ride by in her van. It has a rack on the back that I recognize. She makes my tail wag. She likes to hug me and I like the way she smells. When she passes by, I squeak and cry. If that doesn't get me outside, I start to bark real loud. I have put three holes in two screen doors. I am not proud of that; I just can't control my emotions. Eventually, the Hajinians get the message and let me out. If I can dodge their hand with the rope leash, I escape and run over to visit my dear friend. That's my entertainment. Watching life pass me by.

CHAPTER 18:

Guilty Until Proven Innocent

Armenian Party

Guilty? Me? I was well fed whenever the Armenian relatives came over. This was a loud, confusing bunch. Some noticed me, others talked so much with their hands and feet, they almost stepped on me. One thing is for certain, they can pound down the food and they drop a lot. When I lay in my bed late at night, I dream of people food. I am normally fed dried dog pellets made from some animal by-product with a vitamin thrown in for nutrition. Think about eating the same dried dog food everyday. These Armenian relatives were an easy stare down for hustling food off their plates. I would sit in front of the weakest one of them and stare right into their eyes. My face would show no emotion, but inside I chuckled, as they would eventually catch my emotion as a cute, but starving dog. If they didn't catch on, I'd shuffle my feet a little. Guilt would enter the picture. Soon enough, a cracker with delicious crabmeat would be dropped at my feet. Birthday parties are just great!

We Armenians are not big birthday people. Light a candle, sing a song, blow it out – let's watch the Packers. No major drama. Except today. This is the 80th birthday of Aunt Mary, the matriarch of the whole extended Hajinian families. When someone considers it their job to give advice to everyone all of the time, we give them the title of matriarch. All of the Armenian relatives and their non-Armenian spouses were present. Uncles, aunts, cousins, kids, and even neighbors who saw all the cars and stopped by to see what was going on. Lots of people.

Two large birthday cakes were sitting on the kitchen table. These were not your typical store cakes. These sheet cakes were so big they each had to be carried in a three-foot box. There they sat, smothered in chocolate frosting and candy sprinkles. Surrounding the cakes were the leftovers of a huge Armenian buffet. There were piles of food left over. Trust me, no one is on a diet. A diet is a period of starvation, followed by a gain of five pounds. This crowd was stuffed to the gills. I told my wife that you can never run out of food when you have the Armenian relatives over. It would be paramount to insulting your parents and grandparents in front of their friends. You would truly be considered the village idiot. There response would be swift and merciless. "Five people over for pork chops, and she only is serving five pork chops? Did a rock fall on her head when she was young? What is this Bah-Bomb?!"

When we were first married, Mary Kay would remark, "God, Chuck, can your relatives eat!"

What a great compliment. Compounding this great leftover food pile was the fact that everyone brought enough food to feed a small village. Rule number two: never come to someone's house for dinner without bringing more food than you and your family could possibly eat. That way no one can say, "These people ate all of our food! Don't they have manners? They should have eaten something BEFORE they came over for dinner!"

This a tough crowd. They jostle for position in Mary Kay's kitchen. Secretively, hips bump hips until Mary Kay has been edged out of the control position in her kitchen and my aunts are ready to serve. They hold the high ground in front of the sink, stove and serving trays. Mary Kay gets to stand in front of the toaster. Sounding like street merchants, the serving usually went like this:

"You have to try my rice pilaf," my Aunt Catherine would shout.

"Take two of my cheese *bourags*, Chuckie," another aunt would demand.

A cheese bourag is light, pastry dough filled with brick cheese, butter, and some tiny pieces of parsley to serve as a vegetable. The whole thing is deep fried and absolutely delicious. I would explain to my Aunt Mary that I have high cholesterol and am taking medication. Cheese is not part of my doctor's plan for me.

"What do those doctors know?!" countered Aunt Catherine.

"I know of more people who have lost their hair from all of that cholesterol medication!" another relative chimes in.

Armenians know everything about every kind of medication. Well, no, that is not entirely true. They know someone who takes that medication and has a list of side effects for each one. And doctors? Unless my aunts hand-pick them personally, the whole bunch are just interested in money-making, unnecessary tests.

Why fight it? I take two cheese bourags. My aunt is happy.

When dinner is finished, we all retreat to the family room to watch a ballgame and talk about life issues. For instance, 'whose family had the most money when they came over from the old country eighty-five years ago'. Stuff like that. We are happily bloated.

Soon the noise level reaches the same level as Lambeau Field when the Green Bay Packers score a touchdown. True to Armenian form, everyone was talking. Allow me to clarify that statement, everyone was talking at the same time. A question for the ages: When everyone is talking, who does the listening?

We Armenians have mastered that gift. We have the ability to figure out what you will say before the words leave your mouth. If we find the conversation interesting, we will listen. If we could care less about the point you are about to make, we simply ask you a question that may or may not be related to what is about to come out of your mouth.

Sound confusing? Here is a typical example. My cousin tells his uncle about his gallbladder surgery. The uncle simply has no interest in that surgery, because he didn't have his out yet and instead wants to share HIS story. So, he simply changes the subject to something that he hopes interests my cousin so much that he will not be aware of the verbal slight that has just occurred. Here is how it plays out.

My cousin corners someone and explains, "I just had my gall-bladder out and boy…"

Interrupting, my uncle shouts to him, "Hey, how about those Cubs? Are they gonna win the Pennant this year or what?"

"You're crazy! Those Cubs are going nowhere this year!" my cousin responds.

Thus my uncle wins.

Another warning about my Armenian relatives: they speak the truth whether you want to hear it or not. They will also give you the shirt off their backs. When one cousin of mine lost her job, my father offered to pay their house payments. Yet along with that love comes the frankness of their words.

"You have a pretty face, but you are fat," states my Aunt Mary to a shaken cousin. The proud cousin starts to laugh telling us she could never be anorexic because hogs don't get anorexic!

My Uncle Kay hits my stomach and tells me that I've got to tone up. I look 'heavy' to him. Uncle Kay has had problems with his eyes for over thirty years. He no longer drives a car, but he can tell that I have one more belt loop exposed. I immediately bring up the Cubs and Brewers, and he starts ranting about baseball. I walk away from the conversation and get lost in all the endless chatter that surrounds me.

These are schizophrenic conversations. "So and so did this; where did they get the money for that? Oh yeah, in the 1930's their parents had a tavern." Apparently, if your grandparents had a tavern in the 1930's, you were set for life. There must have been hidden trust funds galore. This was simply due to the heavy drinkers in Wisconsin.

When we have a point to make, we simply talk louder and point a finger at the other person. We laugh, we insult, we show them who's boss! Aunt Mary pulls me aside and tells me that she always tells her sister and my father, her brother, off. "I tell them off and put them in their place. Am I right, Chuckie?" she asks. Before I can get an answer out, she looks at the heavens contemplatively and answers for me, "If I don't tell them off, who will?"

I guess she has a point. This is Armenian family therapy – having a relative remind you of your faults regularly.

In some families, brothers and sisters might not talk for months. In my extended family, we talk with *cousins* weekly. This may seem foreign to a non-Armenian, but each relative truly cares and loves each other. There is nothing more precious for an Armenian than a blood relative, especially when the world outside seems harsh and cold. Hugs and kisses are the norm. So is criticism. Anyone with sharp edges stops coming around or gets those edges rounded real quick. It's like MY BIG FAT GREEK WEDDING, on steroids. Rivaling faith in God, the family is extremely important and dogs are not considered family members.

My aunts are not crazy about dogs. One simple reason: dogs use their tongues as toilet paper. Cleanliness is more important than anything to Armenians. You could be an ax murderer who cheated on your husband, but if you kept your house clean, *who can really fault you?* After spending three minutes looking at our dog, a question would arrive on my Aunt Mary's eighty-year-old tongue: "How long will that dog live?"

"Mary, don't say that. He's a good dog," my seventy-eight-year-old aunt would scold.

"Catherine, I am not saying anything bad, I was just wondering how long they have to still care for him?" Mary speaks defensively.

Sandy accepted this explanation, even though they had her gender wrong. She showed her thankfulness by licking Aunt Mary's leg.

"Ohhh! Don't lick me, dog!!" Aunt Mary screamed.

Sandy sensed their disapproval and headed for the kitchen. While the talk continued, she found her way to the table. Putting her paws on the table and tilting her head, she was able to lick about a third of the frosting off Aunt Mary's birthday cake. Even though the whole Armenian clan was ten feet away, no one noticed Sandy's follies. They were too occupied with the deep conversations.

Not to worry, there was another cake on the other side of the table with a chair blocking its direct access.

Labs are a thinking breed. They are stubborn and will work for hours to get their way. Sandy analyzed the situation and simply pushed her frosting-covered nose against the chair and moved it. Quickly, she placed her paws on the table and began licking more frosting off the second cake.

Peter and Mary Kay enter the kitchen to get the cakes for candle lighting.

We could always tell if Sandy had done something wrong. Her head would be down, ears pulled against her head. She couldn't look you in the eye as her tail curled between her legs. She would walk very slowly, almost as if walking on egg shells. Sandy knew right from wrong. She just couldn't keep herself from getting into trouble. Food now, repent later, that was her motto.

"WHAT DID YOU DO, SANDY?" Mary Kay scolded, as she scanned the kitchen.

Peter was the first to see the missing chocolate frosting. "What kind of cake is this?" pointing to the cleanly licked cake.

"Oh no, Sandy!" Mary Kay shouted. By now Sandy had stopped moving and her soft green eyes began to blink rapidly. Was she going to get a hit on her snout? She knew something was coming.

Stacy comes to her rescue. "Sandy, did you eat that frosting? Oh you poor dog, are you hungry?"

Sandy's head perked up as she slowly unwound from the fetal position. Her tail even managed to wag ever so slightly. *Um, food?* she thinks, forgetting about her just committed trespasses. Mary Kay is furious with Sandy, as Peter dumps both cakes in the trash. She is also worried about the effect chocolate has on the health of dogs. Their hearts can race causing serious problems.

"I'm not going to tell the relatives what YOU did," Sarah scolded Sandy.

Peter goes and breaks the news to the family as laughter and "oh no's" come out of the family room. Sandy escapes Mary Kay's wrath by following Stacy to her food bowl.

"Good Sandy. It's not your fault you ate that cake," purrs Stacy. She pets Sandy while she eats a bowl full of dog food.

Stacy was always the one to sneak treats to me. If I had a will, I would leave everything I own to Stacy. Of course, I own nothing. I sleep where I want and use their blankets. I don't even own a food bowl. But, Stacy has a dog's heart. She understands. She'd give me anything I wanted...well, everything except chocolate cake. That I had to get myself.

We told Dave and Eddi what had happened. Laughing, they told us a story about their one-hundred, twenty–pound, yellow Lab named Dune. It seems that while everyone was occupied at their Christmas party, Dune put his paws on the table and ate every last cookie off the trays before they could be brought out for the guests. Still to this day, Dave can get a guilt reaction out of Dune with the question, "Who ate the cookies?" Feeling remorseful, this huge dog will drop his head, pin his ears back, and tuck his tail between his legs. This occurs to this day, one year after the incident!

It has been proven that all Labrador dogs have a great sense of guilt. This is due to all the trouble this breed gets into. Great family dogs always come up with human characteristics. They have the daily wonderment of children. And like teenagers, they don't speak our language. Perhaps, Dune still remembers the taste of all those great Christmas cookies. They were too good to be legal.

After some quick thinking at the nearly ruined birthday party, Mary Kay found a small pound cake in the refrigerator and placed some candles in it. Turning out the lights, she brought it into the family room with all of the fanfare of a birthday for the Queen of England. Standing, we all sang with full, off-key voices, "Happy Birthday, Auntie Maaary." Not to be upstaged by guilt, Sandy came in and laid at her feet.

CHAPTER 19:

Cruising the Neighborhood

Neighbor buddy

Being the most progressive city in the twenty-first century, Milwaukee set an anti-cruising ordinance. It seemed that teenagers simply drove their cars around and around the main streets with no actual destination in mind. This clogged traffic and caused girls to hang out windows and scream. They did it in the 1950's and 60's; they even wrote a movie about it called *American Graffiti*. Well, now those kids are lawyers, and they would be damned before they let their children and grandchildren cruise up and down the streets. The punishment now: a $120 ticket and simply the embarrassment of others knowing that you had nothing better to do with your time than to drive back and forth on the same old road.

Fortunately for Sandy, there were no police on our street. She had the freedom to cruise anywhere she wanted, and cruise she did. She was a patient dog with keen eyes to notice exactly when a turned head could no longer see her. She simply would lie in the grass and wait for us to look the other way—then boom, she was gone. Houdini was from Wisconsin – Sandy must have picked up his tricks.

One afternoon, I saw Sandy walking up the street with a rope attached to her collar and some strange lady leading her up the block. Sandy had no address on her collar, but this kind lady loved animals and had been watching Sandy wander the neighborhood for years.

We had never seen this woman before. She was quiet and kept to herself. Even her driveway had a haunted feeling to it – dark and crawling with shrubs and trees. None of us took the time to venture down it to meet the woman. No one except Sandy.

Appearances are deceiving. Lynn, I learned, had a kind heart and just loved animals.

"Sandy," she explained, "walked up my driveway. She pushed open the screen door and found me at the kitchen table."

I looked at Sandy as she just stood there looking kind of dumb. Her tail wagged only when Lynn spoke.

"I am sorry about that," I said.

"Oh, there is more," she smiled. "On the table was my lunch, and you guessed it, old Sandy just couldn't hold herself and she ate my sandwich."

Now Sandy's tail was directing an orchestra, back and forth, releasing the emotion she was feeling inside.

"My name is Chuck and I live here. I am really sorry about this intrusion," I replied.

"No, that's okay. I just worry about what kind of owner would leave a nice dog like this to wander the neighborhood. She could get hit by a car. I was just worried about her. It is nice to meet you," she replied as she turned around and left.

This encounter puzzled me. What kind of animal would be brave enough to open some stranger's door, go inside, eat a sandwich off the table, and hang around to kill some time? What was she thinking? Sandy had hope in a stranger she didn't know. She trusted in the goodness of Lynn. Sandy was obviously, unaware of her religion or politics. She felt safe enough in a human's presence to barge in. This was the most natural thing for Sandy to do. I wasn't around during all of her encounters with the neighbors. I am sure some scolded Sandy and maybe a few threw a shoe or rattled a newspaper, chasing her out of their house and yard.

Score that: Dog 'one'. Owner 'zero'. I have to admit after that conversation I was ready to chain Sandy to the garage door. Instead, I bought one of those spiral screws that get twirled into the ground and hold a rope, which is usually tied around the dumb dog's neck. Sandy unscrewed it from the ground by going in the opposite direction of the threads. Dragging the leash and a large metal screw, she escaped again. Despite possible negative experiences, Sandy would persevere. Her mission, to explore brave new galaxies, to go where no man has gone before. Sorry, wrong show. Her galaxy was the fifteen homes on the street where we lived.

I would catch Lynn in her driveway some days. We would exchange hellos. One day, she introduced me to her husband, Steve.

"This is Sandy's owner, Chuck," she explained.

It seemed that Sandy was now a long lost friend, visiting them in their backyard whenever she was in the neighborhood. As menacing as the front yard looked, the backyard was filled with the finest gardens in the neighborhood. I always liked getting Sandy from their yard, as I could catch a glimpse of the colors and fragrance of their laborious gardens.

Steve would confide in me about an old car hidden in a ravine behind his house. No one knows where the bullet-holed 1930's car came from. Dave and Eddi, who were their neighbors, explained that the famous gangster Al Capone stored some of his bootleg whiskey in the barn that abuts their property.

It seems that Al Capone had another connection to our cul-de-sac. His accountant lived in a home at the end of the street.

167

Apparently, old timers remember him coming to his accountant and being rowed across the lake to downtown Delafield for a shave and a haircut. The long deceased barber would nervously shave Al. A slip of the razor could have ended this barber's life. The quarter shave and a haircut was rewarded by a crisp five dollar bill!

I never got a look at the car, but I made some new friends that day.

Sitting calmly on the front lawn while Mary Kay tended the gardens, cars would head to their respective driveways. Cruising at twenty miles an hour, Sandy's head would follow each one when it went by. Suddenly a red mini-van would drive by and Sandy was off. The van was owned by a family who lived two doors down and across the street. Racing up the two-hundred-foot driveway, Sandy circled the van and when Joan got out, she exchanged a hug for Sandy's kisses.

Huffing and puffing, someone was always not too far behind Sandy, yelling at her, "Sandy, bad dog. Get home NOW!"

"Oh, she's fine. Aren't you, Sandy?" said Joan.

The words just left her mouth when Sandy jumped up, paws on Joan's chest, and licked her face.

Completely embarrassed, we shouted, "Sandy, get down," as we scolded with broad swats to her midsection. If she felt the swats, she never let on. She would continue to focus on Joan as if we didn't exist. When she was led away, she would whimper and bark as if she was unjustly being dragged to the local prison and she was being separated from her loved ones. Once inside the house, she ignored our cries of "Bad dog, Sandy! YOU STAY HOME!" She simply raced for the dining room window and looked two-hundred feet away for Joan's car with her tail wagging.

One evening, Sandy was nowhere to be found. It was now night. The kids and I began to walk the neighborhood calling out her name. Sandy loved to hide behind a tree just waiting for us to spot her as she moved from tree to tree. This time there was no movement. After a while, we could hear a faint bark, but couldn't locate the source.

"Where is that damn dog?" I thought out loud. "I have a life besides chasing her around!"

"Dad, she's around here somewhere. You don't have to swear!" explained Kari.

"She probably rolled in some poop and YOU are going to give her a bath, Kari," Sarah reminded.

"I think I hear her voice coming from Joan's garage," Mary Kay announced.

Sure enough, walking up the driveway, we discovered Sandy was inside the garage.

As we rang the doorbell, we discovered that Joan's son had used the red mini-van and that he'd simply closed the garage door without knowing that he had inadvertently locked in an uninvited guest. After apologizing for the interruption, we dragged Sandy home by her collar. She didn't resist and eventually walked alongside of us with her tail between her legs. She knew when she was in trouble.

The very next day, another neighbor was in his front yard and I stopped by to find out how he was doing as he had his house up for sale. He was a kind man who owned a large, male yellow Labrador named Jake. It seemed that Jake was always on a leash and always in the backyard. Sandy would watch Jake standing behind the front door screen and she would tease this huge male by barking at him. Jake was always on a short leash. Sandy would circle around the back by his kennel and just stand there while Jake would bark and run until

169

his choke collar yanked him off his feet. Jake seemed to have ideas for Sandy which were too aggressive for her. She simply wanted to smell, wag tails, and leave. Jake was twice the size of Sandy. His owner had a story for me.

"Our house is for sale. The other day, I threw Jake in the back of my pickup and we went out while the realtor had an open house. When it was over, the realtor told me she locked up the house and let my dog back inside." He shook his head and continued with a laugh, "I explained to her that I had my dog in the truck. When we got home, there was Sandy inside with her tail wagging. She finally got to meet Jake."

What do you say to that? Well, I simply apologized. By now Sandy had made her way across the street and was lying on her back waiting for my neighbor to pet her belly. Apparently, they were now friends.

"Wait, there is more," he continued. "The next day the same thing happened with a different realtor calling me to let me know he let my yellow Lab in the house. Again, Jake was in the back of the truck. This time we knew it was Sandy. Upon arriving home, we discovered that she was so excited that she peed all over our new dining room carpeting."

"Oh no! What did you do?" I asked.

"I called that agent back and told them that they let the wrong dog into the house and they better figure a way to clean this $2600 carpeting," he laughed.

I wasn't laughing when I replied, "Sandy, you bad dog! Gee, I am sorry for all this. I would certainly pay for any damages."

"No problem. We like Sandy," he responded as he petted her belly.

Sandy had a big grin on her face.

As the months passed, we began to hear more stories about our quiet yellow Labrador. Every kid likes some excitement in their lives, a chance to scream and run around. Some have scary relatives that enjoy giving your kids nightmares. Others have a neighborhood dog that lets herself in and then chases around the house as she eats their socks. You guessed it.

"Hey, your dog is over at our house! The kids are having a blast running around picking up their socks so the dog doesn't get them. If you ever go away, I think we could watch her," my neighbor Jim told me.

"How about next week?" I inquired.

"Sure, I'll check with my wife," replied Jim.

Rushing home, I gave the great news to Mary Kay. "Hey, Jim says his kids would like to watch Sandy for a week. Lets go somewhere."

"What are you talking about? You are a dentist with patients scheduled. You can't just cancel them because someone will take your dog," Mary Kay said.

With a mouthfull of breakfast, Sarah splurted out, "You also have us kids."

The reality of my responsibilities sunk in and the dream faded. I called Jim and told him that I would have to take a raincheck on the dog sitting. I also asked him to tell me what that dog was actually doing over there and how she got into the house.

"Well, sometimes she paws at the screen and our son Rick lets her in to the squealing of his sisters, and sometimes the dog just opens the screen door by putting her nose against the partially opened door and wedges it open. Smart dog that Sandy. When she gets inside, she runs up the stairs to hunt down the socks to eat them. The kids scream and have a blast pulling the socks from her mouth. We have three floors and she covers them pretty fast," Jim explained.

"Hey, if she causes a problem, let me know and the girls will come down and get her," I responded.

Sarah, standing next to me in the kitchen, overheard my comments as Sandy kept trying to follow the conversation where her name was mentioned.

"Not me, Dad. Remember the contract I signed?" smiled Sarah, petting Sandy. "Just kidding. I wuv you too, Sandy man!"

Jim continued, "Actually, she is a gentle dog for her size, and it makes the kids pick up their clothes!"

He then went on to explain how he had a dog growing up and how the dog lived to be eighteen years old. Even though the dog was blind and incontinent at that age, when it died he really felt a loss. Sandy was a pleasant reminder of the dog he had as a youth. He invited us over for a glass of wine that night and the dog stories continued. It seems his wife, Pam, had a dog that hung out on the family boat in the middle of Lake Winnebago, the largest inland lake in Wisconsin. One afternoon, while in the middle of the lake, the dog went missing. For a whole day, they searched the lake and shore. As a teenager, that can be devastating to lose your dog. Pam and her sister were beside themselves. Sitting on the dock, they wept. All of sudden, this little dog came swimming ashore and shook the water off of himself right next to the crying girls. It was their dog, Buttons. Well, just telling the story got Pam choked up.

Everyone has a dog story. Those stories are like the warmth of a fire in winter: they make you feel good inside. Dog stories do not involve politics or religion, and this keeps the listener from being defensive. They seem to be ambassadors for those who need a spark in their conversation

One evening, while walking down the street with Sandy and my neighbor Gunar, and his dog Reggie, we were approached by another neighbor, Mary. She told us how she was in her yard on the phone when Sandy came bounding through the bushes and was running straight at her. When Mary was a teenager, a neighborhood dog came running at her and bit her right on the butt. She told us she still has a scar. (Later, I complimented Gunar on his restrainability for not asking to actually see the scar). Seeing Sandy charging toward her brought back bad memories. She quickly ran into the boathouse and hid behind the screen door. Picking up the boathouse phone, she dialed a friend and described what was happening. The friend advised her to stay inside. This girlfriend had just read about how a dog had attacked some woman who was still in the hospital. Some friend!

"Sandy stood by the door with her tail wagging, her tongue hanging out, holding me hostage in my own boathouse," explained Mary.

"She seemed to be smiling at me. My fear went away and eventually I got the courage to come out and pet her," she continued.

Sandy immediately rolled on her back for a belly rub. Mary let out a nervous laugh as she smiled and bent over to pet Sandy on the chest. Just Mary and Sandy on the lawn with the cool lake breezes blowing. Another neighbor won over.

CHAPTER 20:

Eternal

Rest Time

Winter for Wisconsinites is more of a state of mind than an actual season. It is an endurance battle for our souls. By the middle of winter, the sun sets by four o'clock in the afternoon. That is if it is a sunny day. We get about ten of those each winter. This usually occurs after a blizzard where the temperature is ten below zero and there sits two feet of snow for you to shovel. In order to coax us out of our homes and shovel the beautiful snow, the sun comes out. That is our sunny day. Most of the time the sky and surroundings are grey with more shades of grey. If you look real hard, you may notice a little lavender color in the shadows with the grey.

As an impressionist painter, I believe humans need color. Food, lodging, and color. Grey is certainly a color, but it is meant to intensify some other color like red or orange. In the winter, grey intensifies grey. Grey soon becomes our emotion. The dampness, darkness, and the cold begin to permeate our souls. By February, some of us are dealing with what is called "cabin fever". Cabin fever happens to people who are confined to their homes due to the weather. That loosely translates as a general medical term for getting loony by staring at the inside walls of your house. You look outside, sigh, then run to the bathroom to urinate. You begin to hear sounds and your behavior, and thoughts, well, become loony. Others develop the need to sit in front of fluorescent bulbs to combat "light withdrawal" symptoms.

Getting up in the morning and shaving becomes a chore. Productivity at the office begins to drop. Workers seem to be mindless robots. Our hearts long for the kind of weather the rest of the country is experiencing.

About the time you are ready to quit your job and move to Florida, Spring begins to wake up. Like an amnesiac, we soon forget what we have just been through. We fully embrace spring with the similar anticipation of kids in school waiting for the approaching summer vacation.

There is something about spring in Wisconsin. It usually arrives about two months after the rest of the country. Spring is such a short season that if it lands on a weekend, we throw a party. We are like orphan children at Christmas who must wait for the real children to open their presents, then after an eternity of waiting, we get to enjoy their gifts passed on to us. Each day is marked by excitement and anticipation. Even still, spring comes slowly. "The high temperature today will be 42 degrees," states the local weatherman. Forty-two degrees! This is the middle of May! The national weatherman, Willard Scott, is telling us about 75-80 degree weather from the Atlantic coast to California. We don't even have tulips popping their heads above the ground! My wife is from St. Louis, and her family members could not visit us without commenting about our tulips still being around in June. These in-laws loved to rub it in about how everything is green and blooming in St. Louis. My attitude towards my in-laws comments: "At least I married your sister. Give me a break about the Wisconsin spring!" The sad part is, they were right.

One special spring was different. By the end of March, the ice on the lake was gone and the tulips, daffodils and crocuses were in full bloom. The temperature was approaching 50 degrees and by early April, it was close to seventy degrees! The smells of the gardens awakening were in the air. This rich bouquet of moisture-laden air invigorated our winter weary souls. We could actually see and hear the new green growth pushing through the dried brown leaves and stems. The darkness of winter had passed.

Sandy would be so excited to get outside and kick up the dirt. Weather never stopped her from going outside. Snow, sleet, rain, and even when the temperature got to minus twenty degrees and exposed flesh would freeze within minutes, Sandy would go outside to do her "duty" and take forever. She would stand at the door waiting to come in with an outdoor temperature of minus five degrees. When you finally opened the door, she would turn around and take one last look, just in case a squirrel came out of hibernation.

My patience gone, I would shout, "Hurry up! Get in here, Sandy!" figuring that she would freeze to death without my instructions to poop and get back inside.

This spring would be different, however. We noticed our Sandy getting a little more gray over the previous fall and winter. Her once hyper nature was content to lay down and enjoy a good nap. Her bright eyes were tiring. I read somewhere that dogs age seven times faster than humans. By age four, they are entering middle age and have finally slowed down. By seven they are considered seniors.

I did the math: seven 'people' years equaled fifty-six or sixty dog years, or so the experts told me. At fifty-one, she was a little older than me in people years. Heck if I was going to chase cars! I gave up jogging long ago.

My running friends and their doctors told me for each hour you jog, you add an hour to your life. Think about that – isn't it really a wash? If you jogged for two years and added two years to your life, didn't you just waste two years running? Not to mention the wear and tear on your body, all the showers and shoes, etc…?

I was getting akin to Sandy sitting on the couch and relaxing. She would jump up and put her head on my lap. The old rules of staying off the couch went out the window. There were no rules for dogs once they hit fifty in human years. Sandy capitalized on that. Enough with the discipline, now it was time for her to sleep on and *in* the bed. For the first time she was allowed to climb on the couch and maybe when we were gone, sneak into the coveted living room with the oriental carpets. All that cleanliness we coveted before we got Sandy had simply vanished. No, that isn't completely true. A new virtue took over – enjoying the presence of Sandy.

When your kids are young, there is no record of time. Constant action and conversation keep time at bay. The seasons change and children grow up. They are no longer content to hang around the house as friends, a car and freedom rings in their ears. No more chewing gum and sweeping the hair from their foreheads. For once we sit still and notice the leaves rustling against the patio door, only to be interrupted by Sandy walking in from the other room and jumping on the couch, her head strategically placed on your lap. Not all of the 'kids' are gone.

I found myself hugging her and over the years, when no one was looking, kissing her on the forehead. Sure there was a constant battle with yellow Lab hair all over the place, from the corners of the rooms to the sleeves of your sport coats. We even found a Lab hair on the butter in the refrigerator. Paw prints were the norm on the carpets and the tile. Similar to teenagers. Teenagers make messes and just grunt when you come in. They don't even bother to get off the couch.

However, coming home after a tough day at the office, there Sandy would be, waiting at the door. Her whole body wagged and she made you think that you were the best thing to happen to her the whole day. What loyalty and devotion. For anyone with a dog, that is priceless. Sandy began to enjoy slowing down also. Instead of chasing cars, she would be content to sit and watch them pass by. If the car was recognized, her tail would beat the ground. She was finally mellowing and enjoying the view.

We were a week away from a major house remodeling project. Trucks would be coming, walls would be tumbling down, and there would be lots of excitement for Sandy. She loved construction sites. A half block down our street, there was a large home being built. This was Sandy's morning visit spot. Trucks would roll in and the workers would begin their chores inside and out. Sandy would jog down to the site and greet the workers. Since she was out of sight, we didn't get a chance to see her steal lunches or roll on her back for belly rubs. They must have liked her, because she always went back to see her construction buddies and taunt the neighbor's dog who was kept inside.

It was a beautiful Saturday afternoon with sunlight filtering through the early budding trees. You could almost smell the fresh grass coming up.

"Chuck, get Sandy. We need to go to your mother's," Mary Kay called.

Walking to the street, I began to call, "Sandy, Sandy." There she was, at the end of the cul-de-sac walking down the driveway of the construction site about half a block away. She stopped at the end and waited.

"Sandy, SAANNDY," I called. Then the magical word: "TREAT!"

Again, like a catapult, she raced up the street with her disproportionate small yellow-grey ears flapping, tail wagging, and legs pumping as she raced home. Throughout the years, it had always been a joy to watch this dog run. Yellow and tan shoulders pumping, legs and paws pounding the pavement in a synchronous gallop which hypnotized the viewer into just watching her run.

At thirty yards from home, she stopped in her tracks and fell to the ground. *What's this?* I thought.

"Sandy!" I cried out as I ran towards her.

She slowly got up and began to cough. She struggled to catch her breath and walking back to the house, she continued to wheeze and cough. Something just wasn't right. Was something lodged in her throat? While she stood in the driveway coughing, I yelled for Mary Kay.

"Something's wrong with Sandy! Come quick!" I shouted. By now she was laboring to breathe.

Mary Kay rushed out of the garage, petted her head, and murmured, "Oh Sandy, it's okay, it's okay."

Sandy panted and began to cough up blood. I ran inside to call the vet. It was Saturday afternoon – would Dr. Osgood be in her office? The answering machine stated she was on a continuing education program out of state, but left the number for the Waukesha Animal Hospital. I called them immediately and was told to bring her in right away.

Returning to Mary Kay, I explain what the vet had said. Mary Kay, fighting back the emotion, simply said, "Come on, Sandy. We are going bye-bye."

Lifting her coughing head off the concrete, her tail began to wag as she struggled to get into the car. I drove while Mary Kay held onto her in the back. Even though she was fighting to breath, wheezing and coughing, she still wouldn't sit still. Lunging forward, then into the back, tongue hanging out the window and mouth, she was back to her old self in the car.

Mary Kay walked Sandy to the front door of the small animal hospital. Sandy continued coughing and walked right in. This was the place for sick dogs. Two dogs sat in the waiting room just shaking and trembling as the nurse came up to Sandy and called her name to be

182

next. With tail wagging at hyper-speed, she followed the nurse to meet the doctor.

A parade of dogs and other animals came out of the back room, some with bandages, some looking deathly ill. One woman came in with her dog who had disappeared for three weeks. The dog had worms, a cough, and severe bladder problems, which it demonstrated in the waiting room. It shook like it had seen a ghost. Finally, the nurse would invite us back to hear what was wrong with Sandy. The kind doctor explained that there was some fluid in a lobe of Sandy's lung that was affecting her breathing. He couldn't tell if it was blood or fluid. The cough sounded like kennel cough, but the blood sample did not confirm the diagnosis, and Sandy did not have any of the other symptoms associated with it. She also seemed to be a happy dog despite having something wrong with her. He prescribed antibiotics and told us to watch her closely the next twenty-four hours. Leg bandaged from blood being drawn, Sandy coughed and walked past the front desk to the good-byes of the desk ladies. Her tail began to wag as she stopped and looked up, coughing. Same old Sandy, looking for a friend.

Arriving home, we were greeted by Stacy who'd come home from the University of Wisconsin for the weekend. She had bad news. This past week she broke up with her boyfriend of three years. Teary eyed, she told us the news after we got out of the car.

"What's wrong with Sandy?" she inquired. As she helped her out of the car, she petted her wheezing head as Sandy labored to breath.

"We don't know," I replied with my eyes to the ground.

The evening was spent consoling Stacy and keeping Sandy comforted. Kari tried to get Sandy to eat. Her bowl sat full. She wouldn't even eat her beloved treats. There she lay, holding her head up to breathe while occasionally coughing. Stacy slept in the next room on the couch that night as her room had been taken over by her younger sister when she went to college. She fell asleep to Sandy's methodical wheezing and hoarse cough. Our sleep was stabbed by thoughts of Sandy's suffering. Mary Kay came downstairs at five in the morning to check on Sandy. Her eyes focused on Mary Kay as she struggled to breathe. By seven o'clock in the morning, Mary Kay came up to bed and told me we needed to do something. Sandy was just struggling. The whole family came down and hugged her. Mary Kay, who cared for this dog most of the time, hugged and petted her on the head.

This was difficult for Mary Kay. Here lay the dog which *she* basically cared for. She was the one who stuffed Sandy's medicine down her throat so she wouldn't spit it up. She was the one who fed and kept Sandy's water bowl filled each day. It was Mary Kay who took Sandy to the vet for her checkups and worked on her special allergy diet. She monitored her benedril medicine and made sure she had special vitamins, which gave Sandy her shiny, soft, yellow-brown coat. Now, she was helpless to help Sandy get better.

Sandy looked up and saw the sorrow.

Certainly a dog can feel one's emotions. Sandy stood up and coughed as she went to the door to go outside. We opened the door and she struggled to go down to the lake. In her prime, this took about four seconds as she would bound down over four steps at a time rushing to get to the water. This time was different. It took a major effort to travel the seventy-five feet down the steps to the water. Finally making it to her beloved lake water, she was coughing up blood and started wheezing.

Wading up to her knees, she began drinking the lake water. She then came ashore and laid down. The cool wet morning grass seemed comforting to her. Mary Kay followed her down and called for Stacy

184

to come help her back up. The two of them carried Sandy back up the hill and laid her on the cool, backyard grass. She got up and walked over towards the edge of the property, near her black Lab buddy, Reggie, and laid down, again struggling to breathe.

I picked up the walking phone and called the animal hospital as Stacy, Kari and Mary Kay watched her. "Hello, this is Dr. Hajinian calling about Sandy, she seems to ...."

I was interrupted in mid-speech by Mary Kay who simply said, "Chuck, she has died."

Where do your thoughts go when your emotions are battling your logic. My mind recoiled, 'think Chuck', as my heart felt torn apart. In a choking voice, I told the vet that Sandy had just died. I didn't know what to say or do. He empathically told me how sorry he was.

"What should I do now?" I asked with a quiver in my voice.

He told me to wrap Sandy in a blanket and bring her in. They would be waiting for us. Walking over, I stood looking at this dog that gave us headaches and joy all at the same time. She was at peace; no more suffering for breath. Mary Kay came with a tarp and we wrapped her in it. Trying to snap Kari and Stacy out of their disbelief, I gave instructions for lifting her into the car and taking her to the hospital. The ride was silent except for the sobbing and sniffling coming from all of us.

We were greeted by a caring group of nurses who helped us get Sandy out of the car. Tears ran down my cheeks. The nurses were sad and hurt about the whole incident.

So what if a grown man cries? This was a great dog. I shouldn't feel sorry for her, she lived better than most people do in third world countries. Sandy got two lifetimes of hugs and attention.

"So, why are you crying?" I asked myself as these thoughts ran through my mind. I flashed back to my lack of emotion when my friend Dave lost his yellow Labrador, Dune. I couldn't understand his tears at the time, but now I did.

Logic be damned. I cried in the vet's office.

"How can we help you care for Sandy's remains?" the veterinarian asked.

He went on to explain how an autopsy could be performed and the body prepared for burial. For some reason, I made a quick decision, almost reactionary. Arrangements were made to simply dispose of her body. No autopsy, no retained ashes, no burial spot. She was too full of life to be remembered that way. Sandy spent her time all over the place. To confine her to a small grave just didn't fit into my emotional state at that time.

When I left, I thanked everyone and cried on the way home.

Armenians are emotional people. We cry over people, religion, animals, politics and food, and usually in that order. Coming home, I stood there in the driveway feeling extremely lonely. The only place I could turn to on this quiet Sunday morning were my neighbors. They would understand the pain I was feeling. In retrospect, I didn't know much about these neighbors until Sandy introduced them to me. Now these neighbors were there to help me get over my grief. I know Sandy couldn't have planned that, but in a roundabout way, the neighbors helped share our pain.

Unable to fight back the tears as I walked down the street, I took Sandy's bowl and food over to Reggie, the neighbor's black Lab. Ringing the doorbell, I explained how we just lost Sandy. I didn't want reminders of her right then. I could see the sadness form across their faces as tears welled up in their eyes.

I walked up to another neighbor with tears running down my cheeks.

Pam was getting out of her car after church and said, "Chuck, what's wrong?"

"We lost Sandy this morning. She just died," I choked. She hugged me and told me how sorry she was. Her son Rick started to cry, since Sandy was his buddy, too. He would let Sandy into their house each day to wander around and get fed treats of all sorts. Enough of this. I had to get my emotions in check. There was a new members' class at church and I was to be the main speaker in ten minutes. I drove with my red, tear-soaked eyes. What could I do in this condition?

I simply walked in the room with twenty-five adults looking on, and choked back a few words about how my dog had died that morning and that I wouldn't be able to talk with them. Their silence told me they understood.

Arriving back home, silence filled the heavy atmosphere. I was touched by the stillness. There was a total lack of rhythmic noise of paws against the tiles or barking or whining.

Driving Stacy back up to school that same day, we did our best to console her, telling her that she would get over the loss of a boyfriend and a dog over time. Armenians have great advice for dealing with grief: occupy your mind with doing something constructive. That way, when the grief finally leaves, you have accomplished something besides a hangover.

"Concentrate on your studies. We love you," we told her.

This was my hard-driving daughter with a heart of gold. She was the one who pushed for this dog patiently for over four years. A day would not go by without her hugging her dog. She considered

Sandy, *her* dog. She just let her siblings play with her. Now the heart-break of separation had to be dealt with. I guess the Lord does give and take away. Thoughts, no matter how true or meaningful, do not take away the sadness that you feel. You find it hard to concentrate. The gnawing comes in waves. It is hard to explain how attached you can become to a dog until you have lost one yourself.

During the next week, Mary Kay and I would find ourselves sobbing with waves of sadness for Sandy. Some memory would return and then tears. We would comfort each other as we came home to an empty house. Each time, we would expect her to jump on us or try to wedge out the door. Nothing but silence. All this emotion from a guy who, for his daughters, bought ten goldfish and a guinea pig as a 'substitute animal' for a dog. Soon we would discover we were not alone in our grief.

EPILOGUE:

Neighborhood Party: Ode to Sandy Sunshine

Cazador, Mary Kay, Garbo and Dune

Days after Sandy's passing, neighbors stopped by. Some had tears in their eyes. One neighbor who was constantly chased and licked by Sandy simply told us that she could not drive by our house without getting choked up. "I loved that dog more than I love my own dogs," she explained. "She was a permanent fixture on your front lawn, watching the cars go by."

At the office, I would tell my patients that we lost our yellow Labrador. Some could feel the sorrow; others would just listen. Talking made things better.

I e-mailed a friend who told me that it took him three weeks to get over the loss of his Collie. He bawled for three weeks, and I consider him a tough Italian guy!

By day two, the neighborhood seemed strangely quiet. We were so used to having this bundle of energy come running up and down the street. Since so many in the neighborhood were hurting, I felt that something should be done. We decided to have a final party to celebrate our common mischief-maker, Sandy. Invitations were sent to the fifteen families on our street.

I tied a small helium balloon around our mailbox with the simple words, "Sandy Sunshine." This was to be my welcome sign.

Twelve families showed up with seven dogs in tow. The other three sent cards! Others who had cared for Sandy came also. I was truly overwhelmed by the response. I have had fundraisers for Congressmen at my home that had one quarter of the response. The wine and soda were flowing. People food was abundant. Dog treats were ample, and the seven dogs that showed up chased each other around. Each had a blast eating both the dog treats and people food that they could steal.

For us, this was our final goodbye. The neighbors wanted to know why she died being so relatively young. Although we turned down an autopsy on the dog, the vet felt that she most likely died from a ruptured aneurysm or a cancer that affected a major blood vessel in the lung. Surgery would not have helped. I could now explain this without tears. The party was working! I got a chance for the first time to hug the neighborhood dogs. Most were kept inside or in an outdoor kennel. They were beautiful animals, but were kept for the enjoyment of their masters only. I relished the chance to pet these dogs. They all knew Sandy and their ears would perk up when I mentioned her name.

This was our chance to hear things about our dog that only the neighbors knew. What was Sandy doing all that time wandering around the neighborhood? Each took turns telling their stories. Apparently, Sandy would go from house to house on Saturday mornings. The neighbor boy, Rick, would let Sandy in by the screen door and allow her to run around their house. She would be fed pancakes or whatever was available for breakfast. Shortly thereafter, she would head to the next neighbor for sausage or eggs. This was a great cholesterol binge. Always tail wagging, always eyes showing appreciation and, if you got close enough, a big lick across the face. One neighbor told the story about how she was all alone and Sandy pushed the screen door open and came in. She treated her to a tomato sandwich. She loved animals and adored Sandy.

Our neighbor Gunar, who owned Reggie, the black Lab, brought over a large contorted filbert tree in memory of Sandy. Gunar told us about how Sandy would come over when they had company, open the screen door with her nose and paws, and just sit at their guests' feet. The guests would remark how gentle and friendly their dog was. Gunar would have to explain that the dog wasn't his, but the neighbor's! Even their black Lab liked to have Sandy over. A couple of sniffs by both, and they would wag tails together for a half hour looking around for some food or action. To this day, if Gunar wants Reggie to go outside, he simply says, "Reggie, go get Sandy!"

Another neighbor would retell the story of how she would drive slowly past our house so Sandy could catch up with her car as she entered her driveway. When she opened her car door, Sandy would jump up and lick her on the face. Tears were now streaming down her face.

One friend of ours named John, watched Sandy when we were on vacation. John has a big presence. Weighing over three hundred pounds, he has a heart to match. John and his wife would welcome Sandy when we went away. Sandy reminded him of the yellow Labrador dog he and his wife had that had passed away. His dog, however, was the epitome of the highly trained dog. We would laugh at Sandy's disobedience. John always said that all Sandy needed was a firm hand.

"Be my guest," I once told him. "See what you can do."

John would spend lots of time working with Sandy. The results were always the same. Sandy would disobey, roll on her back, and then jump up and lick his face. John would continue to bark commands until his large, red apple cheeks were covered with dog slobber. Obviously, it took more effort to go through that routine than it would have simply been to obey the "Sit" order. That was Sandy.

John told the story about how a young Sandy would want to run all over. He didn't have time to chase her around his large yard, so he simply put a large log on the end of a thirty foot rope. This kept her from roaming. (Later that day she would follow John across the street to a brush fire dragging the rope and log). When you grew up with a dog, it always brings back memories when you watch someone else's dog. Sandy was the perfect medicine for John. He would vigorously rub Sandy's head and ears as he hugged her. Sandy would smile and slobber his big face with licks. She could receive affection and return it.

The stories continued as we watched a perfect sunset on the lake. I finally took the invisible microphone and thanked all my neighbors for all the love they'd given to Sandy. I also thanked them for being tolerant of her obnoxious friendliness.

"Perhaps we can maintain the closeness that Sandy introduced," I suggested. I wanted to say more, but my neighbors' faces said it all.

Sandy broke down barriers which should shame us all. She knew no distinction of person: young, old, male, female, rich, poor, animal or human; Sandy loved all life. She had no distractions, like a job or family to care for; no responsibilities – just to be a dog! She was a dog to the fullest. She taught us that no matter what is on our minds and hearts, each person before us is special. They deserve our attention and interest. How many of our neighbors had their days brightened by her daily intrusions? How many of my neighbors were burdened by problems of illness, job concerns, financial burdens, marital difficulties? We are all tight-lipped. Sandy, for one brief moment, helped them forget their troubles. When they drove by or saw Sandy walking down the street, a warmth developed in their chests. Even my Armenian aunts called to tell me that for a dog, Sandy was a good one.

Wouldn't it be something if the whole world had a Sandy?

We shouldn't need a world war or a natural disaster to make us feel that neighborhood bond. Maybe a lick on the cheek is not in order, but a hug would not hurt. Sandy would be proud.

Hey, I am proud. I am here in dogs' heaven. Actually, that is not completely true; there are other animals here. It seems that anything that had breath on earth and was loved by someone is up here hanging out. It gets kind of crowded at times and some of these animals are pretty weird looking. Heaven cannot be described by me. (Maybe those "meals on wheels" chipmunks could). It is so beautiful, it hurts my eyes. You see, I can finally see *color*.

When the clouds clear, I get glimpses of the family now and then.

Garbo! Great party. Thanks! I saw all those people and dogs at my party. Boy can they eat and drink, and how about those people? That was my kind of party: dogs, treats and people food! It was good to see all the neighbors together. I don't think that ever happened before. They should move in with you and Mary Kay.

My tail wags just thinking about all those stories and treats. I bet Reggie went home and threw up! She could inhale anything. Fastest eater I ever saw.

It is always pleasant here. Sunshine and green grass. No more choking on a leash; I don't even wear a collar. And, I can run anywhere! You can't beat that!

I tell everyone about my family and sometimes we watch. I can't wait for the kids to get up here. Sometimes I can still feel Stacy squeezing me and kissing me on my head. I see that all the

kids, Kari, Stacy, Sarah and Peter, are grown up now and out of the house. They would squeeze me real hard and I would fight to get away – those were playful times.

Hey, I see Garbo is still raking the leaves. You make these big piles and then the wind blows them all over the place! I laugh and laugh. The wind does what I used to do. You would rake. I would scatter the leaves looking for the tennis ball the kids threw into the leaf pile. Remember how you would get angry and yell at me? I didn't care. I am a dog; we just wanna have fun! Have you found the hole I chewed in the oriental rug in the living room I was not supposed to go in?

At times, I knew the family and I were thinking the same thoughts. We had a bond even though we couldn't speak. Sometimes dogs and people get like that. Sure, I miss Mary Kay's walks. I would take *her* for a walk as I pulled on her shoulder, dragging her along. Where was I going to? I never really knew!

Speaking of family, did I mention that my mom and dad are here? I look just like my mom. I've got my dad's nose! Also I have two brothers that I haven't seen since our Ripon, Wisconsin days at the kennel. It has been many years since we were together. Their lives were no match for mine. I brag about all the neighbor friends and family I had. My brother saved someone's life once. I kept geese from pooping on our property. We have lots of tail wagging and stories. My brothers and I stand around with tails wagging in perfect harmony, shoulders swaying from side to side, and tongues hanging out. It would make a good television commercial.

Have I told you that my brothers are good runners? That is true, but they can't beat their old sister, Sandy. We run through beautiful flowerbeds, tearing them up, just like at home. And we chase squirrels, chipmunks, ducks and animals I can't even name.

Up here we just give them a little lick if we ever catch them. So far that hasn't happened. Well, that's about it.

We are having a blast every day. I had a great time with my human family. I shared my love of life with all the neighbors on my block. We all made it a better place to be.

You know, for every lick I gave a neighbor's face, I got two pets on my head. Life is like that. I have got to go. My brothers found some squirrels hiding behind a tree and my job is to flush them out on the right side. Boy, is this going to be fun. See you someday soon. Sandy.

William Saroyan and Michael Balakian are great Armenian writers and story tellers. I am just a story teller. Without the help of the following, this book would just be a long conversation. I am grateful to the following people who gave me a chance to record the history of my now grownup family and Sandy, the lovable family dog. Without the help of the following, it would not have taken place. I thank Jessie Noeblin for her editing and optimism from the beginning. Also I thank Tony Skarlatos who did such a great job with the cover photography. To Peter, Sarah, Stacy and Kari, who had their lives exposed in this book and added critical help from punctuation to grammar.

"Dad, you are not a writer," my English degreed son would exclaim. True, but I tell funny stories. Even he agreed to that. Invaluable encouragement and help in understanding how a dog would talk came from screenplay writer and playwright *extraordinaire*, Mary Strong. A special shout to Ray Robinson at Dog Ear publishing, who took the time to explain how a book gets put together and published. Without his confidence and expertise, the big 'wall' could not have been cleared. He listened and believed.

Finally, a thank you to my wife, Mary Kay, who did all those things I was supposed to do while I was writing this book and for having the courage to get all of us this amazing dog, Sandy.